Letters to a New Generation

Also by Gladys Denny Shultz

Letters to a New Generation

For Today's Inquiring Teen-Age Girl

by
GLADYS DENNY SHULTZ

J. B. LIPPINCOTT COMPANY
Philadelphia and New York

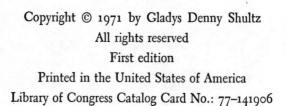

Contents

Introduction

First of all I would like to make it clear that while at the time of researching and writing this book I had two granddaughters in two different colleges and both gave me invaluable assistance, the Janie of the letters is neither granddaughter, and the young people whose opinions I quote came from many different college campuses and high schools in different parts of the country.

These were procured through a questionnaire, made up after consultations with young groups and individuals, then distributed by friends and many others whose identities I will never know. I explained that I wanted frank, uninhibited expressions from young people as a help in writing a book similar to my *Letters to Jane*, which has been used in many high schools and colleges since it was first published in 1947, but directed toward conditions and problems facing young people today.

Replies from girls, both teen-agers and those of twenty and over, considerably outnumbered those from males, but there was a gratifying response from young men twenty and over; and, while that from teen-age boys was numerically smallest, it was large enough to constitute a good sample. The heaviest concentrations of responders were in the East, South and Midwest, but replies came from as far away as Alaska and Hawaii, and from young men in the armed services and from self-supporting girls as well as from high school, college and graduate students.

The ratios of agreement and disagreement in a number of

instances coincided rather closely with answers to similar questions asked by scientific pollsters. However, my own poll was such a random one that I make no claim for the statistics and feel that the value lies in the many thoughtful, perceptive comments and the diversity of views, indicating first that there is no solid bloc of youthful opinion, as one has been led to think, and second that a large sector of our youth has not been heard from in the public pronouncements of what today's young generation thinks and wants. Among all who replied, in fact, just about everything has been said that can be said on the various topics. It remained for me only to indicate with which views I agree or disagree, and my reasons.

I regret that space considerations made it impossible to use every single comment, exactly as stated, for the many individual twists revealed something about the writers and were proof that they were not parroting some shibboleth but had thought the matter through for themselves. I especially appreciated the frankness of those who expressed opinions they might have considered unwelcome to an older person and the friendly spirit and evident desire to be helpful which characterized nearly all. I had taken pains to ensure the anonymity of those who cooperated. Nevertheless a number appended their names and addresses and quite a few wished me luck. I hope I haven't disappointed them too much.

My regret is especially great that I was not able to use more than the tiniest fraction of the excellent expressions by my adult advisers, procured in the same way as those from the young, because of the obligation I felt to be fair in presenting the wide range of thinking offered by those under twenty-five, which I believe will be as interesting to older as to young readers. I am anxious that all who filled out those long questionnaires should know how very helpful their ideas were to me, whether or not I was able to quote their particular contributions.

I suspect there will be people who will wonder, perhaps be shocked, at some of the topics and material in a book intended for teen-age girls, exact age unspecified. In fact, I had suggested to distributors that the young people's questionnaire should be confined to males and females between the ages of seventeen and twenty-five. However, a sufficient number of replies came from fifteen- and sixteen-year-olds to show that matters once reserved for the adult or near-adult years are now pressing upon the middle and in some instances very early teens. Answers to the last question of the young people's questionnaire, which asked if there are areas in the field of sex and morals in which the young are not sufficiently informed and which should be discussed in a book for girls in the late high school and early college years, brought a flood of further subjects which these young people, particularly those twenty and over, felt should be covered in such a book, and is the reason for a number of the topics included.

If a girl has just entered the teens and has not been exposed to drugs and the challenges to traditional morals being purveyed so bounteously by reading matter, movies and in some instances companions, a better choice for her than this book might be one of those listed at the end of Letter XIII. But it might be borne in mind also that a principal charge brought against parents, schools and our society by a large number of these young people of both sexes was failure to give frank and full sex information at an early enough age; and personal experiences related to me by girls as a result of "not knowing what it's all about, though I acted as if I did," warn us that we should not wait too long to acquaint a teen-age girl with facts, as opposed to illusions, about the way one's use or abuse of sex affects one's life.

I am well aware that there may be many, both young and older, who will take exception to some of my own conclusions. They are simply the best I have been able to arrive at after examining the evidence for and against the traditional moral standards and weighing it in the light of the great changes brought about by science, medicine and technology in the last fifty years. I am sure I still have much to learn and shall be happy to hear from dissenters.

My contacts with the young in carrying out this project have made me feel the justice of another charge brought by many: that older people fail to recognize that today's young people are up against problems as difficult for them as our very different types of problems were for us, and that our failure to give valid reasons for viewpoints which appear to them rigid and hypocritical has been no help. If we can't find valid reasons, we should be willing to admit it. On the other hand, we will be hypocritical, and cowardly as well, if we do not stand staunchly by values which our life experience has taught us are essential to the survival of our society and, as matters stand today, of the human race itself.

A much greater difficulty than the probability of making myself generally unpopular is the speed with which events move today, as compared with the time required to put a book through the works and place it before the public. As I close this manuscript in the summer of 1970, I am painfully aware of the possibilities for bad trouble from the explosive polarizations and militant attitudes which have grown up in the last year or two. A Presidential commission has just placed the major blame for the turmoil in the colleges since 1965 on the war in Southeast Asia. If it continues, what will be the situation in the colleges in 1971? If the fighting stops and our troops are brought home, will our government succeed in converting to a peacetime economy without bringing on a depression which will bear most heavily on the young and minority groups? Or will Providence look after us and the crises and tragedies of 1970 be forgotten?

These are questions no one can answer at the moment. Therefore, while trying to give my young readers an idea of the way wars, hard times and prosperity affect lives, ideals and behavior, I have confined myself mainly to the forces which always have been crucial for human happiness and the survival of a society and will be crucial as long as human nature remains what it is.

It is my firm belief that if enough of today's young generation opt for the honesty, fairness and consideration for others that a number have spoken of; are willing to make whatever sacrifices are required to build a better society for themselves and their children; and will work vigorously to place in public office men and women of ability, honesty and devotion to the common good, there can be no doubt about the outcome.

My very deepest thanks again to the many helpers, young and older, known to me and unknown, who have given this book any value that it may have.

GLADYS DENNY SHULTZ
Garrison, N. Y.

PART I

How Did We Get into This Mess, Anyway?

An Exchange:

Where Angels Fear to Tread

DEAREST JANIE:

I'm so glad I stopped by to see you at school! I was hesitant at appearing there in the role of a grandmother with a grand-daughter old enough to be in college, even though she is just *barely* old enough and is a very new college girl. I wondered if in the eyes of the students I wouldn't be classed along with dinosaurs and saber-toothed tigers! What tipped the scales was that I thought you might be a little lonesome and home-sick and could stand some cheering up. But here you are established already with a fine group. And your new friends were so pleasant and welcoming that I felt as though I had sloughed off twenty-five or so years and was back in the time when I used to drop by to see your mother at college—not too often, I hope.

I've been thinking over the question you asked me just be-fore my plane was called and that I didn't get to answer: what differences I had noted between the college then and now. Maybe you were just making conversation, but I was interested in that myself because of all the talk about the "new" genera-tion, so here goes.

[3]

What struck me first, of course, was the way the campus itself has grown and changed. All those handsome new buildings; and, if you'll excuse my mentioning it, the greater convenience and attractiveness of the girls' dormitories. I couldn't help contrasting your nicely furnished suites with the plain little bedrooms of yesteryear; and the lounge in each suite, where boys were free to come to chat or study or for small meetings, with the single big room on the first floor of your mother's dorm which had to do for all social purposes, males being barred from the upper stories unless there was some dire emergency, such as a fire.

I also got an impression that the problems—or perhaps I had better say the concerns—seem to be very different today. Your mother's friends used to let me sit in on their bull sessions and after a while even began bringing their problems to me. These seemed to consist mostly of parents' quirks, questions of dating and morals, relationships and problems with boys. Not that her generation was unaware of or unsympathetic to social problems and those less fortunate. The old missionary spirit still prevailed, and a number were preparing for life work along those lines. But I don't believe they felt obligated to shoulder global burdens while still in college. I imagine your generation would consider them to have been pretty immature.

The burning question on campus now appears to be another restructuring of the college, though there was considerable talk as well about the issues which concern our society as a whole. I think it is wonderful that so many are taking so seriously their responsibility toward their college and the world outside, and particularly admirable that so many are actually working in community or political enterprises. But I'm curious. Don't personal foul-ups exist any more? Doesn't the present generation have any headaches over parents, or boys, or whether or not they'll pass a subject, or what they should do about this or that? I would really like to know.

Thank you again for a wonderful time. And please remember me to Nancy and Marcie and Elsie and the rest.

Lots of love to your dear self,

GRANDMA

DEAR GRANDMA:

I really enjoyed your visit, and the kids have been saying they hoped you would come again. We would all really love to see you.

And do we have problems! Oh, not any terrible personal ones that I know of. How right you were to say I was lucky to have got in with such a good group right from the start. I'll always thank my lucky stars for Freshman Week, when we new students came on ahead and had the campus pretty much to ourselves. That gave our little clan a chance to find each other. We clicked right off and have stuck together ever since. Otherwise I imagine you *would* have found a lost soul, crying for her mommy!

So what's our problem? Well, when the upperclassmen arrived we found out how green we new kids really are, at least our bunch. It's not that the older girls are unkind; most of them are sweet and helpful when we cross their paths. But they seem so sure of themselves and have such different ideas from what we're accustomed to that you feel sometimes as though you had landed on another planet. And it doesn't help that some of the freshmen from the big cities chime right in, and does that ever make us kids from the smaller places feel young and unsophisticated!

I don't know just how to describe it, but you get the impression that everything you were taught in school, and maybe just believed, is the opposite of what is real and right. Like loving your parents, and thinking the U.S. is a pretty good country to live in, and sort of liking school and some super teachers

[5]

and not getting in too deep with a boy friend. They look at you pityingly if you let it slip out that you have any ideas of *that* kind.

We've learned to keep still and not say anything that would show our ignorance. But if you could hear the way we girls hash things over when we are by ourselves, I suspect you would think you were back in Mom's dorm! Except that the college doesn't seem to care what anybody does as long as they are fairly quiet about it.

I hope I haven't upset you, Grandma, and it isn't as bad as I expect I have made it sound. It's just that we're up against some things we don't know what to think about, and we don't like to worry our parents with them.

Hey, I just had an idea. Mom has told me about the letters you used to write to her and her friends when she was in college, and that they really helped. How about some letters to *our* crew? As I've mentioned to the kids, you're really with it, especially for a grandmother. I've told them how you've been a newspaper woman and on magazine staffs and written lots of articles and books and had exciting adventures and are practically unshockable. And about how interested you've always been in children and young people. I feel you are a friend, besides all the other things a grandmother is supposed to be good for, like making the best pumpkin pies ever. I didn't ask my question just to make conversation; I wanted to know, and I believe some of the other kids would like to too. Anyhow, do come back whenever you can!

Lots of love and hugs and kisses from

JANIE

DEAREST JANIE:

That was the sweetest letter! I think the nicest thing that could happen to a grandmother is to be accepted as a friend by one's grandchild. But as to your other kind comments—you mustn't build me up too much with your friends. I'm about as confused by what I read in books and magazines and newspapers and hear over radio and TV as your group could possibly be by the upperclassmen.

Between you and me, I too have gone through a rather rude awakening. For quite a while I went along in blissful ignorance of the generation gap I was reading and hearing so much about. Since compliments are flying around, I must tell you how I hugged myself with delight over the way you kept your head in high school, and the lovely girls who were your intimate friends. The other young people I know have seemed to exhibit just the standard adolescent phenomena, same as the generations before them as far as I could see, and to be working purposefully toward worthy goals. Oh, I hear tales of young people who drop out of school and join way-out groups, and of course I read all the time about marijuana and LSD and other drugs. But these things don't seem to have affected the ones I know, and they have treated me as though I were still a member of the human race in good standing, in spite of the two-generation gap between us.

My rude awakening came when an intelligent, well-bred girl, a college senior, excused and even applauded conduct of a name personality which to a great many people had represented an inexcusable flouting of ordinary decency, in addition to breaking the moral and ethical codes of our society. It developed that she knew nothing about the circumstances of the case, though it had occupied much space in the newspapers only a few years ago, and when I described them she said, "I don't believe it." Then she went on to say that anyway the old moral standards don't apply any more; it is up to each individual to form his own moral code and to act in accordance with it.

You spoke of my being "practically unshockable," and that

[7]

should be true of anyone who for many years has studied human behavior and has been involved with the many kinds of difficulties human beings can get themselves into. I try to look at things from other people's viewpoints and, when I can, to help those who get into messes. But to be calmly told that the rules and values our society has held to throughout the centuries are no longer valid gave me quite a start!

Shortly after that I was told that a recent graduate of one of our famous women's colleges had dismayed older alumnae, met to discuss the college's abolition of curfew and other rules regulating student behavior, by saying that it was no use for colleges to try to protect the girls' virginity because most of those entering college today have already lost theirs while in high school.

It makes one wonder what goes on in the minds of the young people one had thought one knew so well. Are they hiding their real opinions from us older folks, or are the things reported true only of a minority? I had deplored, if not actually condemned, the example set by the name personality. Had I been justified in that? Or was it a sign of hardening of my moral arteries? So I can understand why you and your friends are inclined to keep quiet around people who are sure they know all the answers.

The situation today is so different from any the world has experienced before in so many ways and is changing so rapidly that I doubt anyone could say with certainty what the outcome of some course of action or other would be. However, I will feel privileged to have an exchange of ideas with your group, consulting together to try at least to sort out what is true from what is false.

I would like first, if possible, to learn more about what today's young people think about things in their inmost hearts. Do you suppose you could get your group to answer some questions, to start us off? We could find a way to make it

[8]

anonymous, no one knowing who had expressed what opinion, so the people who cooperate could feel free to be completely frank. Would it be possible to get responses, too, from some of the upperclassmen you speak of? Quite an assignment, I know. But you might ask some of your friends about it, see what they think.

Loads of love,
GRANDMA

P.S. On second thought I realize the girls should have an idea of what they would be getting into, so here are some questions that have occurred to me. You mentioned low regard for parents and schools; I'd like details. I would also like to check some of the things I've heard or read as representing the "new morality," etc. I'm enclosing my list on a separate sheet. Don't hesitate to tell me if you get nowhere with the above. I can imagine that college students are pestered to death with questionnaires, and I will understand.

DEAR GRANDMA:

I'm afraid to think what you must be thinking, it has been so long since I got your letter. But I have been at work, as you will see from the enclosure.

First of all, I showed your questions to the girls I had already spoken to, and they said they would answer them and would pass some out to people they know if they could have some copies. That gave me courage to tackle some of the older girls in the dorm. A few stuck up their noses but most fell for the idea and promised to pass out some to people *they* knew. Then I ran into a senior girl I had barely met who is tied up in so many campus activities I didn't dream she'd have any time, but decided it wouldn't hurt to try. Right off, she said, "Why, yes, I think I can get so-and-so and so-and-so and so-and-so to pass some out." All the ones she named are campus big shots, I'd have you know.

I told Jack—remember him?—what was up and he said, "Why keep it to the girls? Why not let some of us fellows in on it?" I didn't think you would mind, and Jack promised to take a bunch to distribute among boys he knows. So then I thought, "Why not get at it while they're in the mood?" One of the kids has a friend who works in the office, and she got permission to run off your questions on the Xerox machine, and here is what is already going around. As you will see, I said you want the kids to be utterly honest, and that they needn't sign their names, and gave your name and address so they can mail their answers to you directly. I think people kind of liked a chance to be really frank with an older person, without its being taken personally. Several said they'd like to know what you make out of it.

I have to sign off now. A term paper that has to be in Monday is eying me threateningly. Hope the way I set up the questions is all right.

Gallons of love,
JANIE

P.S. Maybe I took more on myself than I should have, but it seemed like a good idea at the time. Anyhow, Grandma, like it or not, you're in business! Will I ever feel like a dope if nobody comes through!

DEAREST RASCAL:

You certainly trapped me neatly! I guess I can't get out of it now, can I? I admire your enterprise, though, and you thought of everything in setting up the questions. I'm glad you asked people to give their age and grade in school and indicate whether they are male or female. It will be very interesting to see if there are differences in the opinions according to sex and age. You can have a job as my secretary any time.

I must have picked up some thought waves from you, for I've been busy along similar lines. It occurred to me, too, that it would be good to get some masculine reactions, and also some from high schoolers and working, noncollege young people. I brought up the matter in the coed high school group I was telling you about, and they said they would help. One senior boy even suggested that I get opinions from older people as well, so as to "combine the freshness of youth with the wisdom of age!"

I thought that an excellent idea. I should reach out beyond my own circle of acquaintances, since like does tend to herd with like, so I've been mailing out a questionnaire for persons over twenty-five to friends in different parts of the country, for them to give out to people they know, who in turn will distribute them to likely prospects. These also are to be anonymous except in cases of a few professionals, whose opinions should be particularly valuable.

You mustn't feel badly, darling, if people lay the list of questions down somewhere and never think of it again. Even a few honest, uninhibited expressions from young people would make the effort worth while from my standpoint. And if not a single one were to come back from your campus, I will still be ahead because our project has opened frank communication and has brought us closer.

Goodnight, sweetie, and all love,
GRANDMA

Editor's Note: The questions for young people and adults mentioned here and in succeeding chapters will be stated in the chapters in which the results are reported and discussed. The original questionnaires, as circulated, are reprinted in the Appendix.

How About the
Older Generation's Morals?

DEAR JANIE AND FRIENDS:

Well, Janie honey, you needn't have worried. Answers are coming in; the mailman handed me a thick bunch of envelopes this morning, saying, "You're getting popular!" I hope this is just the beginning and will reserve comment to see if there won't be more.

My question as to whether you believe there has actually been little change in moral conduct, that young people today are simply doing openly things their forebears used to do *sub rosa*, has brought a question back to me, which I quote:

"You are asking questions about this generation. I would like to give you a little data on the 1930's. My grandmother was teaching in the college where the following took place, and my aunt was a student there at the time, so I know the stories are true.

"1932. Two coeds died suddenly. Investigation showed that both had undergone illegal abortions.

"1933. The daughter of a college official dies as the result of an abortion.

"Another of my aunts was teaching in a high school in the

early thirties in a city where a ring of boys and girls from the best families was uncovered, mixed up in murder, drug addiction, blackmail, sex orgies, etc. The boys were collecting hush money from the girls' families. Also, marijuana cigarettes were being given to grade school children.

"Why aren't such incidents as these brought out by the older people when they speak of the youth of today?"

And in the same vein, a twenty-eight-year-old male Ph.D., who had received one of the questionnaires for people over twenty-five, responds to a question in which I had used the phrase "general moral climate" by saying, "There has never been a 'general moral climate.' Mass communication has only made obvious what has always been true before; in this sense it is providing a useful function by stating the truth."

For the rest, I find an interesting diversity of opinion. The girls under twenty registered a third more "yeses" than "noes" when asked if they believe there has been little change in moral conduct, with such comments as: "Yes, emphatically; it was true twenty years ago but not so openly spoken of," versus "No, people do whatever they believe others do, whatever that is," and "No, it's not what they're doing, it's the feeling they have about these things."

Girls twenty and over give a little edge to the "no" vote with comments of: "No, the change has come about because young people are accepting the responsibility of their actions," "I think there is more premarital sex today, but openness is a factor that makes the increase seem exaggerated," and, "No, today they start younger and are more involved." But there are also "yes" votes, with such comments as, "That is only part, but I think true of many and healthier," and, "The attitude has changed for the good."

Among both male groups the "yeses" and "noes" are running neck and neck, the main comments being with regard to more openness today, with two young men over twenty remarking, "Yes, I think today's youth are more truthful, even if sometimes to a fault," and one who checks neither says he has no basis for judgment, adding, "Probably we are 'less moral' though."

So while I wait for answers to the further questions, I thought I might give my view on this subject. But I wondered how interested you people would be in variations on the theme, "Now when I was young—" Would that kill our project right at the start?

Since I last wrote you, Janie, I have enlisted several young friends of both sexes between the ages of twenty and twenty-five as on-the-spot consultants to augment my high school people. I asked them about this. They said they thought young people would be interested but warned that I must be careful not to give the impression that, since some of your elders have broken moral laws, it is all right for you to do so.

I can't deny that moral standards were broken before your generation came along. I can remember the scandal the senior girl speaks of; it was spread all over the newspapers and rocked the entire country. But I doubt that the members of the ring, if any are still living, are inclined to talk about their youthful exploits. And I would hope that if any became parents, they would have done anything, given anything, to keep their children and grandchildren from following in their footsteps.

The most superficial dip into history will make it plain that the Judaeo-Christian moral code which has been the standard for our Western society has been broken countless times since it was first formulated by Moses some 4,000 years ago. But I definitely disagree with the statement that there is no such thing as a general moral climate, and that mass communication has only made obvious what has always been true. Mass communication has made people aware of instances of crime and immorality to a degree that has never been possible before. But it is not true that there has been no change in behavior and in our own society's attitudes toward infractions of the old moral code. I have seen these changes take place, and members of my generation had a hand in them.

Mine was one of the last American generations to grow up in the moral climate which prevailed in middle-class society before World War I, at least in the Midwest and, I believe, in middle-class society the country over, except for the more sophisticated circles in some of our larger cities.

In our city there was an area downtown where there were saloons and a red-light district, and after my oldest brother went to work on the morning newspaper he gave the family a dramatic description of a visit he had paid, accompanied by a plain-clothes detective, to a house that was the haunt of cocaine addicts—"dope fiends" we called them—and of a red-haired woman who had screamed curses at the visitors. In the early 1920's, when I was Sunday editor of the newspaper, we ran a feature story on the same house, which was still the haunt of drug addicts. But this world never impinged on ours, and drugs were as foreign to our experience as thousand-year-old eggs.

As for premarital sex—when I discussed this with my young counselors one said, "People who don't know you won't believe you." But believe it or not, the truth is that throughout high school and college I never knew of an abortion or illegitimate birth and I never knew or heard of a forced marriage while in high school. I was told of one forced student marriage while I was in college, out of a student population of around 1,500, but I didn't know the couple.

This phenomenon was not confined to the Midwest. A friend who grew up in New England and graduated from an Eastern women's college in 1919 tells me that she never knew of an illicit relationship among her contemporaries while in school, and that none came to her ears until 1930, when an unmarried classmate revealed that she was having an affair with a married man. By then the general moral climate had changed markedly, as we shall see.

The record my young friend was afraid you won't believe was due to the moral climate in the society we were part of. Don't forget, I'm speaking now of the years prior to World War I, which began for America in 1918, the year my class graduated from college, our boys wearing military uniforms underneath their gowns.

It was a highly religious climate, particularly in the Middle West, labeled "The Bible Belt" by H. L. Mencken. Our city boasted of the number of its churches, and the majority of children and teen-agers went to church and Sunday school as a matter of course. It took a lot of courage to be an avowed atheist, or even agnostic, in the Middle West in that day! Whatever one's attitude toward religion, it is generally conceded that, where taken seriously, it is a restraining force in morals. Public opinion polls today indicate that young people from religious homes are inclined to hold to the old moral standards.

These were strict indeed in my day in several of the leading Protestant denominations, the only ones I was familiar with. At this time the church my parents belonged to ranked ballroom dancing, cigarette smoking and games using playing cards (in my home we were allowed to play a game called Flinch, with a special deck) among the deadly sins. Indulgence in alcohol, unless prescribed by a doctor for medicinal purposes, or extramarital sex for any purpose whatsoever, were considered so wicked as to be unimaginable for people like us.

It was understood that engagements could be sealed with a kiss, but that there should be no kissing prior to that, or handling of any kind except for an escort to take a girl's hand or arm when she needed assistance. A darling little freshman girl confessed to me her pangs of conscience because, on a bob-

[16]

sled ride, she had let a very nice freshman boy hold her hand under the blanket.

After one became engaged it was permissible to kiss as much as one liked and for the young man to put his arms around his financée's shoulders or waist and to hold her hand, but that was all. Well-brought-up boys were taught that it was a man's responsibility to shield a sweetheart from his male passions and to break off whatever was going on if sex feelings began to stir.

Undoubtedly there were boys who didn't obey the rules. The point is that they didn't usually try it with the "nice" girls from respectable homes. It would have been prostitutes or pickups, unfortunates from the wrong side of the tracks, lacking parental love and guidance, who supplied their need. But I would guess that a majority of the college boys were as virginal as the girls, and the first Kinsey report, on the sex lives of American males, tends to confirm this. I'm not guaranteeing that no engaged couple, ever at any time, overstepped the bounds. I can only say that, among my acquaintance, weddings were announced considerably ahead of time and first babies appeared at entirely decorous intervals after the ceremony.

But the age of innocence was soon to be no more. You probably have heard and read a good deal about the flaming youth of the 1920's—girls first leaving their iron-maiden corsets in the cloakroom at dances, then discarding them altogether; boys spiking the punch at college parties; boys and girls together breaking loose from supervision by their elders and ranging far and wide. Somewhere in there, I don't believe the exact date has ever been pinpointed, petting became a part of casual dating and we began to hear of abortions in some high school sets. By 1930, a very nice girl, a sophomore at my own alma mater, was telling me her woes. "The boys don't even take you to a movie any more. They just drive to some deserted spot and park, and from then on it's a battle."

[17]

Fiction of the 1920's described the "flapper," as the new type of girl was called, in novels such as Floyd Dell's *Moon-Calf* and others by writers now forgotten, and F. Scott Fitzgerald got much of the material for his short stories and novels about the "lost generation," a name later given to it, from studying his wife, Zelda. She began flaming, entirely on her own, while in her mid teens, before we got into World War I, and at the age of thirty began the series of hospitalizations for mental disorder which continued until her tragic death. A recent biography of her, *Zelda*, by Nancy Milford, in my opinion gives the best picture yet drawn of the "beautiful people" of the 1920's.

The flaming youth of course were a new young generation. But I have to admit that it was not only youth that flamed in the roaring twenties. Young marrieds and not-so-young marrieds got into the game. I'm not referring now to my college friends but to the adult society of our city and of cities over the country. We women had been given the vote, hobble skirts had disappeared along with high-buttoned shoes, and hemlines retreated to the knees. One heard tales of respectable matrons throwing up or passing out in the middle of a ballroom floor, from too much liquor. There was a good deal of flirtation, most of it not meant to be taken seriously. But it was rumored that at big parties there was a certain amount of carrying on by husbands with other men's wives, in cars in the parking lot, just like the young folks. I can't say which group began it. The divorce rate began to rise at such a pace that Judge Ben Lindsey, of the Denver Juvenile Court, proposed that couples should try out "companionate marriage," by living together for a period of time to see how congenial they were, before taking their vows.

The people I'm speaking of were not members of high society or of its lower levels; they were respectable middle-class folk, who had been reared in God-fearing middle-class homes. That they had broken away from childhood teachings was due to the appearance on the scene, almost concurrently, of elements never present in American life before which were to make a considerable difference in the customs of my generation and the ones that have followed us.

World War I began it, stirring up emotions and wiping out forever the safe, dependable world in which my generation grew up.

A second factor was prohibition, made the law of the land just after World War I. I heard veterans complain bitterly that while they were away, fighting for democracy and freedom, a minority had taken advantage of wartime preoccupations to slip prohibition over on their fellow citizens. Many who hadn't gone to war were indignant when they waked up to what had happened. People began drinking who had seldom if ever used liquor when it was legal, and getting around the law became a game of wits.

A third factor was the large-scale production, by an assembly-line process, of inexpensive cars, Henry Ford's contribution to technology and the sex revolution. When I was in college no student had a car, and friends who attended Eastern schools tell me that none there did either, except for a handful of sons of very wealthy families. On rare occasions one of our boys might be permitted to take his father's car for a special date or excursion, but most of the time we either walked or took the streetcar—another reason why it wasn't too hard for my college generation to observe the moral code.

Fourth was the lessened influence of religion. Darwin's theory that mankind had developed from lower forms of animal life had gained acceptance over the Bible's story of creation. This was a heavy blow at the divine nature and authority of the Scriptures. With "the Bible says" no longer holding good for many who had feared hell if they sinned and hoped for Heaven if they didn't, there was a loosening of morals as well, to the anguish of my parents' generation.

Fifth, by this time Freud's work had become widely known,

and the theory that emotional and mental ills are due to sexual inhibitions was the basis of the greater part of psychiatry and psychoanalysis.

A sixth factor, and a very important one, was the hitherto unprecedented prosperity that followed World War I. Industry was booming and the stock market was shooting up at a rate that reminded one of Jack's beanstalk. Hordes of "little people" were buying stocks on margin, paying 10 per cent down, then sitting back and watching the stocks make them rich.

Hollywood was rolling in money, and the movie colony ran wild. Sex scandals were a dime a dozen, and there were even murders, never solved but rumored to have been caused by sex imbroglios. One very popular young male star died from drugs. The films also were becoming more and more risqué, until the church people rose up in wrath, a "czar" was appointed to regulate the movie industry and morals clauses were inserted in the contracts of the actors and actresses.

Here I must make it clear that by no means everybody took part in the high jinks. For one thing, the great majority of Americans still lived on farms, and farm people in general have always been more conservative than city folk. At least, they were until television began to bring its burden of crime and violence into rural as well as city homes. Also, agriculturists did not share in the general prosperity, and Middle Western farmers in particular were hard hit after European farms went back into production. You may wonder why I go into this dull economic stuff. It's because there has been a very real connection between money and morals in the social changes since 1920.

One can only guess what might have happened if the expert economists of the twenties had been right who were assuring the American public that we were entering upon a golden age of prosperity, having reached a plateau from which the only

possible route was up. (One leading expert was warning that
the bull market wouldn't last forever, but Cassandras never
have been popular and few listened to him.) My own guess is
that if it had not been for the Great Depression we would have
arrived at the excesses of the late 1960's much sooner than
we did, but I could be wrong. A great many people had simply
gone along with the merrymakers, not joining in the didos
themselves but not wishing to appear to be wet blankets. I
know that the tolerance of some of the onlookers was beginning to wear thin before the stock market crash occurred in
October, 1929. We of the class of 1918 were in our thirties then
and had started our families. A friend told me about a party
she and her husband had given not long before. They didn't
patronize bootleggers, and two of the guests, knowing this,
had each brought a gallon of wine.

"The party got pretty noisy," she told me, "and around
eleven o'clock one of the guests suddenly made a dash for an
open window, stuck his head right through the screen, and
vomited! He wasn't a drinking man, he hadn't realized he was
taking too much, and he was terribly embarrassed, besides getting his face scratched rather badly.

"One of the bachelors, I'd say in his early thirties, had
brought a college girl whom we didn't know. When they said
good night, he picked up a suitcase from the front porch,
where he had left it. I said, 'Oh, are you going somewhere?'
He looked a little funny and said, 'It's hers. She's going somewhere.'

"It seemed odd for her to be starting out on a trip at that
time of night, and after everyone had gone I spoke to Bill
about it. He said, 'Didn't you get it? They were going on to
a hotel.'

"Fortunately Sally had slept through the whole thing, but
before long she's going to be aware of the way the grown folks
are behaving. And I didn't like the idea of a college girl going

from my home to spend the night with a man. Bill and I talked it over. We are not going to have any more of that kind of thing in our house."

The depression had a sobering effect on nearly everybody. A number of people who had been on the verge of divorce stayed together because they couldn't afford two establishments, and they remained together. The rates for marriages, births and juvenile delinquency also went down. When people are scrambling with all their might to keep a roof over their heads and food on the table, they don't have much time or energy to play around. And even after things got moving again, the economy never really recovered, the administration having to keep "priming the pump," pouring more money into public works and such, until World War II came along.

There was some general and very wet rejoicing when the prohibition amendment was repealed early in the Roosevelt administration, but people calmed down after that. We had seen what had happened to some of the freewheelers of the twenties, and I think most of us had decided that the old moral standards, rid of silly pruderies and secrecies of the Victorian era, were best.

However, some consequences of the 1920's remained with us. The bootleggers and rumrunners who had been put out of business when liquor was made legal turned their organizations and talents to promoting gambling, prostitution and drugs, founding the crime syndicates that have muscled into legitimate business and politics and now form an underground empire second in power only to our Federal government. And the custom of petting remained, creating problems for girls from the 1920's to the present day.

Let's skip along now to the early 1940's. Recently I heard a psychiatrist say that this was when the sex revolution began—evidently he wasn't around at the time of World War I. But the second great conflict did start it going again, through the disruptions of our populace and the river of money the government began to pour out to defense industries; and it went right on as our country became the wealthiest the world has ever known, and the barriers that had imposed restraints on speech and conduct began to fall one by one.

In the late 1940's the first Kinsey study reached a wide general public, in spite of being published as a scientific study, and it quickly headed the best-seller lists. We became accustomed to seeing four-letter words written out in novels about World War II, as we had become accustomed to seeing and hearing swearwords in novels and plays about World War I. The practice of steady dating among young teen-agers began with the Korean War in the early 1950's and, added to petting, has been responsible for many forced marriages, illegitimate babies and abortions in the younger groups.

In the 1950's also, Professor Timothy Leary, an unfrocked Harvard professor, started a new religion based on the use of hallucinogenic drugs. It began to be fashionable to take at least one trip on LSD, and I needen't mention what has happened about marijuana. Supreme Court decisions made it possible to publish and sell openly works of literary merit, such as *Lady Chatterley's Lover,* heretofore sold only under the counter, and movies became much bolder. Then, in the middle 1960's, a Supreme Court decision exempted from the definition of pornography any work having the slightest social or literary value.

Since then we have been inundated by a flood of sex of every description, along with violence and defiance of authority of any kind. We of my generation look on aghast. Was *this* the result of our rebellion against the pruderies and prejudices of our parents' generation?

However, the important question is: Where do we go from here? Maybe, as our exchanges continue, together we can begin to make some sense out of the crazy mess we're all in.

Janie, some more questions have occurred to me. Do you suppose that you could get your people there to go more into detail about the new moral code? I've made out another list, just in case.

Please thank for me the people who have cooperated so wonderfully.

My best to all,
GLADYS SHULTZ

PRIVATE, FOR YOU ALONE, JANIE:

I have just reread my letter, and I'm not sure I ought to send it. What will your friends think? Will I disgrace you? I said I would answer questions, and I would hate to renege. But I would rather do that than gloss over the facts with a lot of platitudes. I'm going to leave it up to you. If you think the effect would be harmful, just mail it back to me and we'll forget about the older generation's morals.

GRANDMA

DEAR GRANDMA:

Well, I showed your letter to the kids, and it sort of blew their minds. But honestly, I think they believed the first part because you came through on the rest of it. Marcie said she hadn't expected that your letters would be so exciting. Now we're all wondering what you're going to say next. The new questions are going around. Oh, I nearly forgot. The kids wanted me to tell you that when they said those things about parents, they weren't thinking of grandparents!

Love,
JANIE

The Trouble with Parents Is—

DEAR JANIE AND FRIENDS:

I imagine you are beginning to be anxious to know what people are saying in response to other questions in our opinion poll, and the flow of answers to the first group of questions has slackened to such an extent that it looks as though about all have come in that are going to come in, so I'll start with answers to my question about the most serious mistakes of parents, generally speaking, and procedures of your own parents that you will try to avoid with your children. I wish I could report every comment, but you've cooperated so generously that it isn't feasible. So I'll summarize, with some verbatim quotes to illustrate. Age and sex seem to make some difference. I have therefore separated the returns for teen-age girls and those twenty and over, and have done the same for the boys. Here goes, first of all, for the most serious mistakes of parents, not necessarily your own.

In every one of our categories I find the same mistakes of parents in general stressed over and over—notably overprotectiveness, not being sufficiently understanding, too closed-minded, stereotyping all youth in the image of the worst element, hypocritical, too lenient in some things and too rigid in others, failure to communicate, and not loving their children enough.

[25]

Among the girls under twenty, three of these qualities run neck and neck for first place and they are: (1) *overprotectiveness*. "It drives parents apart from children, causes bitterness." "They don't give children enough personal responsibility for their actions and the children therefore want independence when they haven't yet understood what responsibility is." (2) *Not understanding enough.* "To know when kids are up or down and when they can't take a lot of hassling." "Applying conditions of their own youth to situations today, ignoring the tremendous changes that have taken place." (3) *Either too strict or too lenient.* "Too strict because of the drugs, sex excesses, etc., yet some are too lenient, don't care and let the children do what they want."

While voicing the same complaints as the foregoing, the girls twenty and over rank first a charge that parents have failed to give an adequate and honest idea of sex as "something not evil but also something not to play with; developing a real communication, not just shoving a book at their children to read about the 'facts of life,' " as one expresses it.

Replies from teen-age boys are more scattered, covering the same areas as those of the girls but with no particular favorite. But among the young men twenty and over there is most stress on overrestrictiveness. "Parents tend to be unreasonable and bull-headed. Often times they will not explain (or can't) the reasons for rules and punishments and tend only to exert authority. Most youths are reasonable when parents are reasonable." Another cites "resentment of offspring's independence, inability to allow for values foreign to their experience," and still another, "conservativeness—the inability (or unwillingness) to give their children credit for having ideas which they (the parents) could do well to emulate, instead of necessarily demanding that the opposite always be the case. They are wrong in always demanding respect for one's elders, especially when they find themselves cornered, and for being so self-righteous in general."

The teen-age girls add such things as: "Not placing enough trust in their children," "introducing liquor too late," "great pressure on higher education when girls aren't sure they want it," "pushing their own ideas on offspring—i.e., if a guy has long hair they want it cut to make him more presentable to *their* contemporaries."

Further complaints of girls twenty and over are that parents in general aren't honest with their children and "haven't enough discipline, letting the kids run the family"; of not instilling worthwhile beliefs and of not practicing what they preach; of overindulgence ("They give us everything but teach us no respect for things and then wonder why we aren't more appreciative"); of "intolerance and hence of fear."

Both sexes twenty and over place considerable stress on parental materialism. "They have become too devoted to 'things' and fear that these things will be taken away from them by others. They distrust too many people and love too few—if they can 'love' at all." "Many parents I have seen have become so materialistic and oversocialized that they refuse to understand why their kids do what they do. They wouldn't care to find out why kids riot on campus or they think it's just terrible if a child smokes marijuana, because it is against the law and 'they' say it will lead to use of heroin and other addictive drugs." And, "They place the emphasis on material success rather than on interpersonal concerns."

Now for the procedures of your own parents that you will try to avoid. But not all parents are guilty of the faults of parents in general, as is shown by the fact that at least one tenth of you can think of no procedures of your own parents that you'll try to avoid, and several express deep appreciation for the kind of upbringing they've had.

For the rest, parental overprotectiveness got the most votes among girls under twenty, expressed variously as "setting hours to get in," "imposing morals," "not letting kids make mistakes," "not letting the youngster take the responsibility for himself and others in the family," "worrying too much." But a sixteen-year-old says, "I wouldn't try to avoid it, but I would tighten up a bit on letting my children date while still young and letting them out so much. Because my mother lets me out a lot and I feel free to do things I shouldn't."

Here is a heterogeneous assortment of complaints: "Commanding obedience without giving reasons," "trying to mold youngsters to fit into their own socially acceptable world," "lack of understanding or interest in what is most important to me at this time," "prejudice against guys because of race or religion," "doing things to embarrass their children, making us feel insecure," "giving us too much money," "I will be more understanding when my child gets into trouble at school," "less formality, my own home will be more uninhibited," "nonacceptance of deviations from social standards."

Then there is a scattering of the kind of unhappiness which arises from tangled family relationships: "Don't involve children in parental disputes." "I would be more fair to all the children and more lenient with older ones." "I will avoid my father's tendency to jump to conclusions about kids and not give them a fair chance. I will emulate my mother (who died recently) who was always 'one of the kids,' which was wonderful." "Arguing in front of the kids, discussing financial problems. Children should not be bothered with these until they are older." "Attempt of one parent to dominate."

Only one girl in the teen-age group complains that her parents haven't been "frank about sex," but this is the leading complaint about their own parents by girls over twenty, as it was of parents in general, one girl saying, "My parents never told me anything. I had to learn the hard way and I am very bitter about it." Others speak of hang-ups about sex, of instilling guilt feelings about it, avoiding the subject and "giving their children the idea that it is dirty."

A number say they will try to communicate better with and be closer to their children than their parents have been with them. Several will hope to avoid a "tense atmosphere," or yelling and loudness and "the harsh fights of parental separation and the insecurities this might cause." A number also mention lack of understanding, coldness and refusal to "accept their children as anything but dumb kids," while one wants to keep from "making my child feel guilty toward me and being afraid of the young."

One girl, by contrast with the teen-ager who thought her father was too harsh, says that what she will try to avoid is "being too lenient, with too few rules, mainly true of my father. I'd rather be more strict, as my mother was, with specific rules, such as curfew, for them to follow." Several say they will spend more time with their children, and one will avoid working outside the home, as her mother does. Still another will avoid giving her children *too much* (her italics). "Let parents and children share something besides a house and three meals—an understanding where love can follow." And a third will abstain from "giving the children too much without requiring them to earn some of it."

Several of the boys under twenty criticize their own parents as being either too strict or too lenient, which were leading complaints of parents in general, and others give, as procedures to avoid, "faltering in making a serious decision, thus appearing unreasonable in the eyes of those who rely on them," "rough talk," "pushing kids to a certain pattern in life—they should be allowed to experiment," "cruel and unjust punishments," "their prejudices," and placing "restrictive work suddenly on children. Such things should be planned ahead."

The young men twenty and over stress, as did their feminine

counterparts, inadequate sex instruction—"my kids will know and have it"; narrow-mindedness—"I will stay away from cemented prejudices"; arbitrary decisions "made out of consideration of social attitudes"; and more freedom for the children to make their own decisions. Several vow that they won't worry as much as their parents do.

Other procedures to avoid are refusing to discuss a problem with a youngster; ignoring questions which are unpleasant or embarrassing; narrow, traditional adhesion to moral and other standards; and "being overawed by one's children." One young man gives "my mother's attempt to psychoanalyze us all"; another, "the attitude that the kid is the 'crown of creation'"; a third the need of his parents "to know *everything*, their inability to respect their childrens occasional desire for complete privacy, to be let alone. I would not make any children of mine (over eighteen) divulge personal matters that they choose to keep to themselves. I would ask if they needed my help but would not press unless they wished to confide."

Well, now we know! I appreciate the kindness of those of you who exempted grandparents from blame. Nevertheless my generation raised the parents of your generation, so we must accept our share of the responsibility for whatever may be wrong with them.

It's evident from the many different types of charges you have brought that parents come in many shapes and degrees of adequacy or inadequacy, as has probably been true of parents through the ages. To try to deal with all the different foibles of individual parents would be an impossible task. I think my best service will be just to tell you how your parents may have been affected by the New Enlightenment which burst upon the world in the 1920's, and the events following it.

And now this rummaging through long-buried memories is beginning to hurt. At the time, we of my generation had thought we were so right in replacing *our* mothers' methods with new "scientific" ones, and later we found out that in many ways we had been so misled!

For there was a revolution in childbirth and child care in the 1920's, along with the religious, technological and sex revolutions. Around 1900 the medical profession set itself to cut down the number of deaths of mothers and babies in childbirth, a most laudable goal, but again with results that no one had anticipated.

The members of my own generation were born at home, in our mother's bed. As soon as we had been tidied up a bit we were placed in her arms, to be snuggled and cooed over and comforted after the long, hard ordeal of the birth canal and the harsh expulsion from the warm, cozy dark. Many of us while tiny slept in our parents' bed, or else beside it in a cradle set on a stand so that it could be gently rocked to a mother's lullaby. When hungry, we had only to cry to be put to our mother's breast.

I don't know the exact date when all this began to change, but by the 1920's when my college generation started our families, babies of middle-class parents were born in hospitals, and we, the mothers, were often so heavily anesthetized that we didn't know when our babies were born or were given only a glimpse of them before they were whisked off to the hospital nursery. Here they lay alone—and still do, in most hospitals— in separate cribs, being brought to the mother at four-hour intervals (in that day) for feeding only.

And it went right on after we took our babies home, supplied with four-hour feeding schedules and strong injunctions to ignore the baby's cries between times, aside from checking to see if a pin was sticking or a diaper change was indicated.

I shan't go into the whole gamut of since-discarded theories by which we enlightened mothers of the 1920's, with the best intentions in the world, bedeviled our small folk, following the instructions of the new experts. Later, still other experts were to attribute many personality problems of your parents' generation to those methods, and the pendulum began to swing back toward more humane procedures. By the 1950's, in fact, it had swung back so far that much of the mother lore of my parents' generation had become the new best way, carried in some instances, as a number of you have mentioned, to the point of letting offspring raise themselves and run their homes and parents.

And the ill effects of the more idiotic theories of the 1920's about baby care were offset to some degree by help from the new science of child psychology, which was trying to find out what small folk were really like. As in the therapy groups so popular today, mothers in groups set up for the study of pre-school and older children learned that other mothers were having the same problems and also became acquainted with the kind of behavior that was normal and natural at different stages of development, including curiosity about sex. It still seems to me that the conscientious, reading, studying mothers of my generation did a pretty good job with sex education.

However, there were some side effects to the new knowledge of child nature that my generation was acquiring. In my young days, fathers were figures of authority, whose word was law as long as youngsters lived under the parental roof. But in the 1920's the mother began to be the dominating force in the family, partly because of the trend to city living, with the father absent all day, and partly because it was the mother who read the books and articles and conferred with the pediatrician, and hence felt that she knew best.

Then pretty soon mothers began to get it. I believe it was in the late 1920's or early 1930's that we entered the great debunking period. The saintly character of motherhood was challenged by various writers, and later the word "mom" was attributed to possessive, dominating mothers. So that the reading, studying mother, when moved to require certain things of her youngsters, was inclined to wonder, "Am I being a mom?"

Let's go back now to the Great Depression, which I'm told you are all sick of hearing about. As one of the young men has put it, "It must be remembered that the depression really has no meaning for us. When parents refer to it in the sense of 'You kids have it easy; when I was a kid in the depression—' they are in many ways showing themselves ignorant of the problems which young people are having today."

But one of the girls in the twenty-and-over group has put her finger on the cause of at least some part of the materialism of which a number of you complain when she gives as the most serious fault of parents in general, "A materialistic orientation in bringing up their children, due to their having been denied many material things. As a result the younger generation has rejected the upbringing in many cases."

That doesn't explain the whole of the present materialism, but I know how important it has been to many of your parents' generation to give their children the comforts and advantages they missed out on in the 1930's. It is the motive which has impelled many a father to "sell his soul" to a corporation, to work to rise in business, to make more money. I am thinking of one darling couple, neither of whom got to college. During the worst of the depression the father of one had work one day a week, the father of the other had no work at all. The couple can't imagine now what their families lived on. The husband has had vicissitudes in his own business, but they have been able to finance a degree in medicine for their only son, and it is all they ask of life. The most grievous hurt of those of my generation who lost everything and scraped along on a bare subsistence level was that they couldn't give their children the things they wanted them to have.

Parents are still like that. The first concern of a father laid off from a well-paying job when the defense plant where he was working shut down was how it would affect his four children. "We are living on my savings now," he told a reporter. "If I don't get a job pretty soon I won't be able to send my children through college."

I have some thoughts about parental preoccupation with college, mentioned by a number of you as a chief parental mistake, which I'll save for another letter. But I'll say here that I agree with charges a number of you have made of handing out too much money, not making youngsters responsible for their actions and not requiring them to earn in some way the extra luxuries they crave. I have been appalled myself at the allowances some teen-age girls are given, figures as high as $20 to $30 a week having been quoted for pin money alone, the parents supplying all needs.

But before we judge too harshly, we might inquire into the motives for the overindulgences. If they are given as a substitute for love and interest in the child, they are indeed lamentable. But there might be parents, humiliated in childhood at not being able to participate in activities of their peers, who wish to spare their children that humiliation. In these cases the overindulgence is still lamentable, but more understandable.

We of my generation were lucky in that the great commercial exploitation of the young didn't get into high gear until our children were grown and had children of their own. To be sure, this also had started in the 1920's after radio had opened to advertisers an audience which didn't have to read to get the message, but it was mainly confined to pushing different brands of cereals, which we bought anyway. It wasn't until the tremendous prosperity which began with World War II, together with the advent and spread of television, that advertisers waked up to a great new field of potential customers, teen-agers with money in their pockets and an increasingly powerful voice in family expenditures. All manner of enterprising adults set out to cultivate this market, with such success that, according to an ad for *Seventeen* magazine in March of 1970, "although teen-age girls make up only 12 per cent of the total female population, they account for 22 per cent of all female apparel purchases and over 20 per cent of all female cosmetic and toiletry purchases. And they spend one out of every four dollars of their families' food purchases!"

By no means has all of this been bad. But the over-all result has been to weld adolescents into a peer group, with loyalty and conformity to contemporaries rather than to parents and the adult society. And it is reaching into ever younger ages, with preadolescents now being flattered and wooed and dextrously alienated from their parents. The latest development is special dress departments for girls from ten to fourteen; one store with such a department does not allow mothers to go in it with their daughters. And apart from all this, the youth cult developed in the 1960's, which purportedly holds up to scorn not only all persons over thirty but all their works and ideas, does not engender in persons forty and over any great amount of confidence in their ability to guide the young.

Truly, my dears, if you knew all the things your parents' generation has had to contend with, I think you would join me in feeling grateful that so many have turned out as well as they have. Your replies to my question about procedures of your parents you will try to emulate indicates that many *have* turned out very well, and I'd like to go on to those next.

It's a list that I wish with all my heart your parents could see, and other people too. Not only would it go a long way toward restoring parenthood to the position of honor it once occupied, it could also provide valuable insights into the kinds of parental attitudes and behavior which promote love and mutual friendship with the young, a subject on which there has been a good deal of adult soul-searching of late.

A nineteen-year-old girl, a college sophomore, takes the prize for brevity by writing, in answer to the question about parental procedures she will try to emulate, a single word: "All." Among the rest of the teen-age girls, the parental quality getting the most votes is showing their love and affection through "creating an atmosphere of love," "loving and respecting my kids, not spoiling, not strict; talking with them, knowing them, letting each learn and grow as his personality leads him."

The next most highly prized quality appears to be freedom, "a fair amount" or "wherever possible," expressed in different ways, such as "letting us make our own decisions," being "reasonable about dating, curfew and week-end trips." A large number of both teen-age girls and boys mention freedom to talk with their parents on *any* topic, with a fifteen-year-old girl, a high school sophomore, speaking especially of her parents' "never avoiding sex questions. I recently asked what the hose on the hot water bottle was for. My mother answered quite readily, 'For douching.' I knew what douching was but didn't know how it was performed. So that little episode, which took about ten seconds, cleared up something I had been wondering about for two months or so." Another girl speaks of her father's "understanding of people, his acceptance of my maturity," as factors in the freedom he allowed her.

There are a number, on the other hand, who stress "firm but understanding discipline," and one girl lauds a "balanced routine in the home, giving the children the stability and security that come from knowing a good dinner will always be ready at 6 P.M. and that a hot breakfast will always be prepared," a sentiment with which I heartily agree.

From teen-agers of both sexes comes further evidence of the respect the young can have for parents who don't hesitate to act like parents: by "not spoiling and by inculcating good manners," "showing what is morally right," "inspiring youngsters to work for high goals, but if a child fails, comforting with love, understanding, interest," by "their attitudes I have learned

[36]

and their manners I've been taught," "having us go to church every Sunday," and "stern but fair discipline," the last two statements being the contributions of teen-age males. Appreciation is also expressed for "encouraging individuality in their children," "knowing their faults, trying not to pass on their prejudices," "keeping children out of parental fights but not denying that they occur"; and one teen-ager mentions parental encouragement of reading and political activity.

The home background described by a teen-age girl might well serve as a blueprint for successful parenthood. "I will try to emulate my parents by making available books, music lessons of all kinds, and their policy of noninterference in the children's lives except when they are doing something wrong. Even then it was the attitude and not the deed they questioned. I'll try to emulate their telling me exactly how they felt, thus keeping misdemeanors from building up to a point where love is inhibited."

Love and affection in the home also get principal stress from young adults twenty and over, expressed by girls as "the love between my father and mother, their ability to settle disagreements peaceably, their desire to give of themselves to help others" and "loving and understanding my children and treating them as individuals with rights, not objects to satisfy the needs of adults"—a very acute observation.

Young men in the older group say they will strive to "create an atmosphere of love and respect": "I'll love my children and knock myself out to raise them 'right.' "

Both the older groups, again like the teen-agers, place great store by openness of communication, being able to discuss anything with their parents, and appreciate having been trusted and allowed as much freedom as was possible. In addition they mention the good example set by their parents; being given explanations and reasons for parental actions and decisions; parental participation in some sports that the chil-

[37]

dren enjoyed. One young man approves his parents' policy of "setting firm guidelines but at the same time developing independence and self-reliance in their children, though being always available if their help was needed."

The young men and women show more appreciation of parental stress on education and willingness to provide it than the teen-agers do, and they place considerably more emphasis on discipline, rules, training and character-building procedures than the teen-age group, taken as a whole. Girls twenty and over express this as "creating responsible individuals," "instilling a willingness to work hard," "teaching values of culture, love and security," "having the children keep to a curfew and giving them strict rules to follow," "making children, boys too, learn to do such things as wash dishes, even though you have a dishwasher, learn to sew, etc." One girl says flatly, "My parents were fairly strict and I believe in it. Many times children are not mature enough to make responsible decisions, so the parents must do it for them."

In addition to voicing sentiments similar to those of the older girls, a rather surprising number of the older males plunk for old-fashioned virtues we are being told are out of date and for old-fashioned discipline as well. One says, "My father was a stern disciplinarian and I intend to be the same." Others cite parental traits of common sense, thrift and honesty as things to emulate. A college graduate praises his parents for "having made us children financially responsible. 'If you want it, go out and earn the money to get it.'"

A college man now serving in the armed forces lists the following qualities and methods of his parents that he will try to emulate: "Using corporal punishment; interest in knowledge; setting of standards; my father's way of achieving success by working toward goals he had set long ago; his example of honesty and correct living for as long as I can remember, and his ability to provide for his family in a way I would like to do. God knows I've been in my share of trouble, but no matter how serious the trouble or problem, both my parents have always stood beside me, their love never diminishing, and this has enabled me to come through."

It is perhaps significant that so many of my older cooperators of both sexes, looking at the matter from a more mature vantage point, feel that they profited from parental methods which involved training and discipline, setting of standards and giving responsibilities along with freedom. Parents who have been afraid of their offspring, as several of you suggest—and, I think, with some validity—might well take courage from this.

Finally, despite some repetition I can't resist sharing with you two more blueprints for successful parenthood, contributed by girls from the twenty-and-over group. Says one: "I will try to emulate my parents' setting up of the family as a unit, to which each member is responsible for his part; with respect, but not subservience, to parents. I will try as they have done to stimulate decision-making, self-confidence and independent behavior. I will love my children, listen to them, respect them, let them be kids. I will punish the behavior, not the child." And the other: "I will try to emulate the good communication between my parents and myself, not afraid to admit mistakes, not hypocritical; their living by professed beliefs while teaching us basic respect for the beliefs of others. Their not being afraid to discipline us, their always letting us know that we are loved."

Answers are pouring in now to the further questions I asked about boy-girl relationships, drugs and the like, and these have brought more questions to my mind. Could I impose on you to answer one more batch? The enclosed will be the last, I promise you. I can't tell you how much I am learning from your responses. Thank you all, again and again.

GLADYS SHULTZ

Have We Oversold Education?

DEAR JANIE AND FRIENDS:

I'm really overwhelmed by the way so many of you are sticking with this question marathon I seem to have been conducting, and by the honesty and frankness of your replies to the questions about moral attitudes and behavior among young people of your acquaintance. I'd like to hold off on these last until all of you have been given a full chance to respond—I know how studies, papers, outside activities cut into your time for such indulgences as answering questionnaires! So if it's all right with you, I'll proceed with your answers to my question, "What is the most serious fault of education?"

Educators should be glad to know that our system has at least three friends among the younger generation. Two male teen-agers wrote "none" after the question about its most serious mistakes, an eighteen-year-old college sophomore adding, "I think it's great!" A girl in the twenty-and-over group says, "Some schools are working out their problems well."

But the rest of you have brought in a bill of complaints so long and varied that it makes one wonder where so many of you got the ability to think and express yourselves so well.

I'll give the charges against high school education first, as filed by teen-agers of both sexes. Teen-age girls put the grading system at the top of their list of faults, a number mentioning "pushing for grades" and others, emphasis on grades rather than achievement. Too rigid and structured a high school comes next: "doesn't encourage creativeness and developing the students' own ideas and interests." Then comes obsolete methods, "too slow for our dynamic minds." A seventeen-year-old high school senior thinks students should only be required to attend school for major subjects, and another believes that "people can learn more than teachers think. Scholastic Aptitude Tests are the most *absurd* and terrible indication of what students are capable of. They must be changed and improved." Further complaints are: too much stress on college admission, not enough responsibility given to pupils, and lack of honor systems; according to one girl, the worst crime is "attempts to make us all the kind of person I particularly don't want to be," and, to another, "stress on producing an ideal citizen capable of adjusting to society rather than an individual capable of changing society."

Boys under twenty also complain of obsolete teaching methods—they don't keep up with latest ideas"—and lack of incentive to learn, "too much homework that has no practical value," and educators who are "in some cases too liberal, as allowing disturbances, and in some not liberal enough"; while a fifteen-year-old high school sophomore's complaint is that "they will not let students participate in the running of the school. Schools would *greatly improve*."

A number of girls twenty and over also feel that the educational system is "too standardized and rigid, lacking practical training" and not progressive enough, but several think it is too liberal. Other comments are: "A twenty-to-thirty-year cultural lag for many young people," "courses unrelated to the interests of teen-agers, that they will never use," "outdated, not related to the real world," "memorizing instead of developing the students' understanding and abilities," "too much emphasis on picky trivia," "requiring students to major in some-thing," "teaching us ideals which never seem to be viable in the real world, for instance, integration and 'all men are created equal' "; while one girl objects to its "not preparing one for a specific goal but giving an over-all wishy-washy education with-out any real value." Still other shortcomings are: "Too separated from life, everything brought into the classroom instead of using resources that are relevant to the student" and "It should stimulate more original thinking."

Many stress pushing for grades, as the teen-agers do, one remarking, "I know many a kid who got great marks while in college but had no social life. Some kids are better at 'bull-shitting' than others, and it is the school's fault for thinking that tricky multiple-choice questions show how much a kid knows. The whole testing and marking system has to go." And a number cite insufficient individual attention.

Some of the older girls mention teachers who "don't care," "aren't interested in their pupils," "can't relate to their class and hence gain the pupil's interest," and are "lazy—it's mainly read the book and learn for yourself"; "college instructors are interested in research and not in teaching."

Writes one girl: "White middle-class schools, through a mass-education orientation, emphasizing discipline and per-petuating the value system of the society, are stifling creativity as well as learning in many cases. They are producing an alien-ated youth in the sense of being unable to express themselves and be heard through the proper channels."

The young men twenty and over also speak of a "rigid, didactic approach in education which doesn't allow for creative stimulation"; of teaching methods that "are dreary and boring; there needs to be a new life and reason to want to learn"; of lessons that are "still a matter of memorizing and not of learn-ing how to think"; of being too competitive, "with no true in-terest in knowledge"; and of not providing sex education.

Another charge is: "It turns out someone who plays the game of responding with what he believes will elicit a favorable reaction," and still another, "the poor who want college can't afford it, the rich abuse it. Hence discontent."

I am sure there is validity in a great many of these criticisms. I myself have deplored the multiple-choice questions which have replaced written work to a considerable extent and to my mind are something of a damper on original thinking and creativity. But I suspect that the charge made by the young man over twenty of turning out "someone who plays the game of responding with what he believes will elicit a favorable reaction" has always been true of a certain number of students and always will be true, and I understand that a number of high schools and colleges are taking steps to give pupils more responsibility and more of a voice in decision making, which is all to the good.

One criticism that surprised me was the statement of a girl in the older group that young people are unable to express themselves. It seems to me that today's youth is expressing itself all over the place, and very ably, too. I have heard many on panels and in radio and television interviews, and surely never was there a generation so articulate.

So many of you are giving the kind of education one should seek after high school as a principal question before teen-age girls today that I'll start my end of the discussion with higher education. One of my young advisers asked me how my college generation compared with the present one. My first impulse was to reply that we were less demanding and more accepting, and that is true. But as I have thought more about it, I have realized that our acceptance wasn't due as much to meekness as to the very different circumstances then. First, prior to 1920, college was a privilege, reserved for the very few. In 1900 only 17 per cent of the younger generation were finishing high school, and before 1920 less than 8 per cent went to college.

Second, to enter a four-year liberal arts college, which to me is higher education or the start toward it, four years of Latin in high school were required, and in some colleges more Latin, and sometimes Greek, in order to graduate. And third, many who attended the Midwest colleges, at least, had to earn all or part of their way. These factors taken together tended to single out those who had a real thirst for knowledge and were willing to swallow anything the college handed out.

And I believe that most of those who elected liberal arts did so not with any idea of becoming rich in a material sense but rather as an opportunity for enriching the mind and life through an introduction to the knowledge and wisdom accumulated through the ages. Indeed, prior to 1920 the better educated—college professors, ministers, school administrators, doctors—had small chance of getting rich, nor had they acquired their education for that purpose. They were looked up to in their communities along with the banker and the leading merchants. All they asked in monetary terms was an amount which would enable their families to live decently. They got their reward through the help they were able to render to their fellow men.

Like most other things in our society this situation, too, was due for a change after 1920. There began a gradual erosion of the so-called humanities—subjects like languages, literature, history, philosophy, concerned with human beings and their behavior—in favor of the so-called natural sciences—physics, chemistry, biology, zoology and the like—the first step being to get the classics requirement abolished.

I do not claim that everyone should study Greek and Latin, though it has never hurt anyone that I know of. Excellent translations are available of all the extant writing of the great Greek and Roman philosophers, poets and playwrights, and plays by ancient Greek and Roman dramatists have been hits on Broadway in recent years. The drawback is that persons with a bent for the natural sciences tend to have little use for the "dead" past, its history or wisdom any more than its languages, and are not greatly interested as a rule in the problems of human beings and society.

This is not true of all natural scientists, to be sure, and a number have suffered pangs of conscience over the way science and technology have disrupted our human concerns. But since 1920 higher education has tended to become more and more pragmatic and "relevant" to the expressed needs of the oncoming generations, which more and more have been to prepare for some line of endeavor that brings higher renumeration than do mere scholarly pursuits.

Higher education, in this sense, was given a tremendous boost by the G.I. Bill, following World War II; quite naturally veterans, some of whom had given as many as four or five of the best years of their lives to their country's service and many of whom were married, with babies coming, wanted to make up for lost time and tended to elect fields where financial rewards were greater.

A further shot in the arm for science and technology was provided by sputnik, in 1957, which so shook up our citizenry that it became a patriotic duty for colleges to produce more physicists, chemists and mathematicians and to turn over their laboratories to research for the defense department and space effort. For a while, liberal arts colleges that didn't convert forthwith into technical schools were on the defensive.

I have a vivid memory of a Sunday evening in the Sputnik era when the president of Harvard was put on the grill by Meet the Press because his university was among those which had resisted the trend. The high point of the interrogation came when a member of the panel let fly with a question that went something like this: "Come on now, Dr. Pusey, tell us—how many boys are going to Harvard today *just for the sake of learning?*"

In addition to the defense and government contracts, there was an increase in the practice of defense and other industries to send employees to college, paying their way, and of sending recruiting teams to college campuses; and a proliferation of scholarships and of bank and state and government loans to finance college for those whose parents couldn't afford it, until by 1970 close to 50 percent of all high school graduates were entering college. A B.A. had become a requisite for landing almost any kind of white-collar job and an M.A. or a Ph.D. a necessity for many higher-echelon jobs.

And science and technology had come close to sweeping the board. The National Science Foundation has estimated that the number of scientists and engineers nearly doubled between 1950 and 1965 (results of the G.I. Bill and of Sputnik combined). A number of these people, it's true, are engaged in social or other humanitarian lines of work. But in 1962, two thirds of the Ph.Ds given were in the natural sciences, with more than a quarter in chemistry alone. The social sciences— those concerned with studying and possibly influencing human behavior—had only 7 percent of all Ph.Ds, and of these economists, who are concerned with the material side of our society, outnumbered sociologists 5 to 1. Need we be surprised that science and technology have run amuck and that our society has become materialistic?

No one has believed in higher education more strongly than I have, or tried more earnestly to persuade young people with a capacity for college to avail themselves of it—though I have urged it for the inner, personal satisfactions that come with greater knowledge of human nature, society and history, rather than for the greater earnings it is supposed to afford, which is the lure still being held out to dropouts, to induce them to go back to school.

But of late I've begun to wonder. The public institutions are swamped by student bodies of 25,000 and upward. New buildings go up on every inch of campus space and overflow into surrounding neighborhoods, sometimes to the indignation of the student body the institution is trying to serve. Competition for "name" professors rivals that for star athletes, leading to a stress on publications they can list rather than on classroom performance and making graduate work in many cases a mockery. I have heard stories of administrative processes breaking down under the strain, staff people grown rude and indifferent. And most disturbing to us who have people we love among the younger generation is that with the great influx of students in the late 1960's bombings came to college, violence came to college, vandalism came to college, arson came to college, and in some places murder came to college.

As I look back over the years from 1920 to the present time, it seems to me that higher education's big mistake has been in its very attempts to be "relevant" to the changing desires of oncoming generations and to make the shifts demanded as social, economic and political conditions have changed.

C. P. Snow was among the first to show, in his book *The Two Cultures*, the process by which education was diverging in two directions, the humanistic and the scientific. In the late 1950's I heard Admiral Hyman G. Rickover haul our educational system over the coals because, when he wished to build the first atomic submarine, he had trouble finding enough highly trained physicists to do the job. As we all know, not just one atomic submarine but a whole fleet of them got built anyway, and enough highly trained physicists showed up to land men on the moon. In the spring of 1969, the same Admiral Rickover was expressing himself as troubled by the ease with which purveyors of technology were pressuring the general public into letting "so-called progress" alter their lives, and stating that our country must learn to control technology and shift to making better use of our natural resources.

And in early 1970, Dr. Barnaby C. Keeney, former president

of Brown University, was warning Congress that the imbalance of science teaching and research in relation to the humanities which is "dividing the nation, destroying its values and making it impossible to solve society's most serious problems" must be corrected or our society is in for real trouble. "It is my own conviction," he said, "that until the electorate and the persons they elect can use historical and philosophical material to help decide the major questions of the day, we shall not solve these problems."

That was precisely what Harvard's president told the panelists on Meet the Press in 1957, but who listened? One of the great ironies is that it was the very efforts of colleges and universities to do what was demanded of them in the 1950's to keep our country out in front in the space and armaments races which brought down on them some of the most violent condemnation of the young generation of the 1960's.

Much of the "grade pushing" so many of you complained of, and which I understand now extends down into the elementary schools, has been due to the eagerness of parents, or of pupils themselves, that offspring should get into one of the status colleges or graduate schools whose degrees have a special value in terms of job procurement and social status and hence are applied to by anywhere from three to seven or eight times the number of people they can accommodate. Yet one can get both an education and the individual attention so many of you feel the lack of in any one of the thousands of smaller and less well known four-year or junior colleges sprinkled over the country.

It seems to me the real job to be done on higher education is to find a way to relieve the liberal arts colleges of the swarms who come in order to be able to make more money, or to get a husband in the higher income and social brackets, or because parents insist on it. As a young man in the twenties-and-over group expressed it, "My dad didn't get to college. He did all right without it, well enough in fact so that he figures if he had just had a college diploma he would have ended up as president of General Motors or American Telephone and Telegraph. So he is determined I'll get mine if he has to drag me through college by my ears."

I am not the only one who has been wondering whether, by our very emphasis on higher education and making it so easy to attain for so many people, we have come close to ruining it. Dr. Irving Kristol of New York University has suggested in an article in the *New York Times* Sunday magazine section that students should be required to pay the full cost of their education, where necessary being granted loans which they will have to pay back after they graduate. Today the high tuition and other charges of the most expensive private colleges don't begin to cover the cost to the institution, and the rates at public universities and colleges aren't a drop in the bucket; the taxpayers, many of whom never had the benefit of college, have to pick up the tab.

Dr. Kristol believes that having to pay for what they are getting would force students to "take a more serious and responsible view of their reasons for being on campus. One does get the impression that for many students the university is now, like the elementary and high schools, a place for compulsory attendance and that the occupation of a campus building is a welcome lark and frolic."

I think that if I were a high school girl today, with no very clear conception of the kind of further education I wanted, I would ask my parents for a sabbatical year or two for making up my mind, especially if I would be under eighteen when finishing high school. In fact, I did stay out of school for two years after graduating from high school at sixteen, and it was probably the smartest thing I ever did. I have known many high school graduates since who profited from a year or more in a job or from getting secretarial or other training in the interval.

There are a number of skills, at present in demand, which

call for short training periods and will enable you to earn something toward whatever further education you may decide on. And there are still fields to which talent and skill are the open sesame. This is true, in fact, of any of the arts. A young friend of mine turned down her father's offer to send her to any college she wished to go to. She had been studying dancing and dramatics for years, looking forward to a career as an entertainer, and this is one of the fields where talent, personality and hard work are all one needs. "I can get further general education from reading and special classes," she told me, and I'm sure she will.

A friend of mine who is a well-known author was asked by a lady what kind of courses her son, who wanted to be a writer, should take in college. "I'm not able to advise you about that," he told her. "I never finished high school." This man had a gift for writing and became proficient simply by writing and writing and writing until at last his stories began to be published.

Don't get me wrong. I'm as strong as I ever was for college for those who want to increase and broaden their fund of knowledge or to enter one of the so-called learned professions. But the way things are today, I believe that about the greatest contribution you can make to higher education is to stay away from college as long as you don't really know what you expect to get from it.

Turning now to education in the lower schools, there will always be room for improvement there, and educators are the first to admit it. It seems to me, however, that many critics fail to take into account the tidal wave of babies born during and after World War II which began to hit the public schools in the early 1950's and kept right on coming, swamping facilities in the same way that colleges began to be swamped some years later; and also the attitude which has grown up as social problems have multiplied that education is the cure for all of them, those of society and individuals alike. It has led to dumping upon the grade and high schools the responsibility for combatting all the evils of our society and for offsetting every shortcoming of all the millions of parents.

I have known a host of dedicated teachers and of many noble efforts to make learning an exciting and pleasurable experience and to develop individuality and creativity, often in the face of resistance by school boards, community members and in some cases parents. If what we are being told is true, that the present young generation is the brightest, the best informed and best prepared of any in our history—and I'll go along with that—someone must have been doing something right.

I hope that your generation, as parents, will assume more personal responsibility for the development of your children's character and potential, work with the schools rather than against them, and help with youngsters whose homes can contribute nothing.

As for "relevance" to current trends and desires, it appears from what has been going on to date that our schools and colleges would have to be switching curricula and studies just about every year to keep up with rapidly changing interests. Yesterday's "relevant" can be irrelevant today and by tomorrow grounds for rioting.

I have noted of late a slight tendency by dissatisfied groups to set up schools or classes where they can be taught exactly what they want to learn, and this is all to the good. I don't know why today's bright young people shouldn't assume the responsibility for things they want outside the stated curriculum and believe they will profit more if they have to raise the money to finance them.

And what is to prevent bright students from developing their individual creative abilities, original bents and interests on their own? I know a young fellow, not yet twenty, who decided when he was eight that he was going to be an architect. Grade schools haven't yet begun to offer courses in architecture, but that didn't deter him. He haunted libraries, read everything about building and design he could get his hands on, and by the time he was fifteen had become so knowledgeable that he attracted the attention of a famous architect, who has been giving him summer employment ever since. One of my twenty-and-over girl cooperators preparing to teach in the grades, writes, "Over and over you hear high school and college kids say that they're tired of having things handed to them on a silver platter. They want to have an environment in which they are free to experiment and make mistakes, but with limits that can be broadened as they can handle responsibility. That is the way I hope I can run my schoolroom and my home, when I have children."

And countless opportunities exist today for high schoolers, as well as college students, to get outside the world of the classroom. There are exchange scholarships with students in many foreign countries and group travel plans, at amazingly low cost, which use hostels where American boys and girls can become acquainted with students from many countries. Your help will be gladly accepted by local hospitals, political groups, volunteer programs of many kinds. The best preparation for changing a society is to find out first what the society is really like.

Meanwhile, I've been acquiring a valuable education myself in your replies to my questions about morals and such. If nobody else gets any good out of this exchange, I am receiving an enlightenment that I wish I could share with all other adults. I should like, however, to finish with the general mess we're in while on the subject. So I'll impose on your patience to take up next your analysis of the most serious mistakes of our society in dealing with the young; then we'll tackle the questions you have listed as being the most serious ones confronting teen-age girls today.

Very best,
GLADYS SHULTZ

Society and the
Younger Generation

My question about the most serious mistake of society in its attitudes toward and treatment of the young really stirred up things! The count of indictments here is again long and varied, and not a single responder had a good word to say for any aspect of the present scene.

Some of the complaints are so contradictory that well-meaning adults who might wish to use the list as a guide in correcting society's shortcomings toward youth could get pretty confused. For instance, a considerable number of you stress too much regulation and repression, while an almost equal number charge society with "guilty permissiveness," "allowing the young to step on it rather than guiding youths so they will be able to make constructive rather than destructive changes," and "being too indulgent and forgiving, so that our morals have lost their true meaning and respect has lost out." Older people are accused on the one hand of rigidity—"inability to think outside the established patterns of values, life styles, actions and roles"—yet I am told on the other hand that too many members of our society "are too liberal and don't crack down on the young when they do something wrong."

However, I find that three principal complaints are made over and over. First is hypocrisy. "They [the older generation] impose a double standard and condemn things the majority did themselves, such as premarital sex"; "society is much *much* too harsh, condemning us for the same type of revolt they carried on in their young days, maybe not as radical but of the same nature."

Next in order comes society's stereotyping all the young as bad—"filth" was the word used by one boy, a high school sophomore—and treating all alike, though several recognized that the drug use, sex freedom and rioting of a sector of youth had been largely responsible for creating this image. The feeling was expressed in a number of different ways. "If society would only recognize that we're *not* all alike." "Why can't they see the good in the young and highlight that, the way the bad is highlighted?" "They should look at us as individuals and treat us like individuals."

The other major accusation is failure of the older generations to communicate with the young and above all to listen to what youth has to say. "Society tells the young they are or have been wrong. If it re-evaluated the areas the *young* call wrong instead of ignoring us or demanding that we come up with something better, perhaps a better relationship would result. It is the older generation that has taught us most if not all we know."

Ranking just under these three is frustration because society doesn't make a proper use of youth but instead "dwells on its weaknesses and scorns or actively inhibits its strengths." As one respondent put it, "It [society] tends to look down on the young. Children are not given a chance to prove themselves." Another: "It fails to realize that seventeen- to nineteen-year-olds (and above) are rational beings who want to help in areas where they see lack of correlation between ideals like 'Love one another' and 'Thou shall not kill' and what society is doing."

[54]

And still another: "It regards young people as a threat rather than as a valuable potential help in solving problems. Less preaching and more teaching would help, also more understanding and less feeling threatened on society's part."

Scattered charges include: constant pressure to conform to the adults' past experiences and modes of dress; resentment of the young, distrusting them, being contemptuous or patronizing toward them; bossiness—"we don't try to run their lives and morals, yet they try to tell us how to run ours"; making the young a separate group; overpublicizing and dramatizing the young rebels—"recognition of this type of behavior is highly detrimental"; inconsistency—"alternately treating teen-agers as children and then using them as adults—a high voting age but a low draft age"; "looking to the appearance of youth instead of to their minds"; and maintaining a medieval family structure— "children should be sent out into the world much younger."

A girl in the twenty-and-over group brings a blanket indictment: "Our society's attitudes perpetuate a system of hang-ups about sex as well as about becoming adults who lead meaningful and fulfilling lives. From early years children are constantly told, through actions and words, that they must work hard (that is, find the right cog in the wheel of capitalism) and postpone pleasure, to succeed. We are punished for individualism and deviation. Communication with adults is discouraged."

Even more devastating is a comment that "they [society] think our generation is very sick, yet theirs is so sick that we will inherit their problems and ours."

And so, I am told by one of the young people, "The American teen-ager is *bored!*" and by another that because society "is involved so much in its precious standards (set by its parents' generation) that any change is looked down upon, it is agreed to be a great big farce by most youth today." I am warned by a third that "Society must wake up to the fact that young people are people and the 'establishment,' those over thirty, must accept the fact that morals and values are broadening."

Two of you delved more deeply, to pinpoint the underlying reasons for society's maladies and youthful discontent. A young man from the twenty-and-older group comments: "Increasingly as students go through high school and college, they become impatient with society, in part because they know that they themselves will have to live with all the ills of society, especially with the population threatening to make this planet unlivable *in thirty years! ! !* We see that to be able to live a decent life thirty years from now we must start taking drastic steps *now* to solve our problems, but that society and our leaders are just dillydallying and threatening *our* future."

A nineteen-year-old college girl also cites overpopulation and pollution as society's worst faults. "I feel they comprise the most frightening problem and are the cause of all problems, really, war riots included; indirectly, but still the root of them all."

I sympathize thoroughly with youth's resentment at being stereotyped in the image of the hell raisers among you; one would need only to read the responses most of you have made to my questions to realize how far from the truth that picture is. I think it might please you to learn that the image of older people as being uniformly resentful and censorious of youth may be equally erroneous.

I don't know if Janie has told you that I have been circulating a questionnaire among people twenty-five and older, friends distributing copies to friends who pass them out as they see fit. Replies have come from adults ranging in age from twenty-five to eighty. These people show a great concern about the state of our society, and its effect upon youth.

In replies to questions designed to elicit their attitudes, they

[56]

were nearly unanimous in agreeing that the "sit-ins, drug experimentation, wanton destruction, repudiation of traditional moral and sex standards and challenges to authority are confined to a few."

Agreement and disagreement were more even—with a slight edge for agreement—on a statement that the youth revolt has been wholesome and good and forced on the young because their elders won't listen. However, two guidance professionals, one a father and the other a mother of teen-age youngsters, both stated that the revolt was good but questioned some of the methods used, and another mother of teen-agers, a college teacher with master's degrees in two different fields, was emphatic in her approval. "The revolt is *good;* some of our basic principles *needed* to be challenged. Those responsible are the most idealistic and conscious of moral values of any group of young people produced in a long while. *However,* they lack realization of the sacrifices of individual rights necessary for such a society as they envision, and their weak awareness of the need for *logical* as opposed to *emotional* thinking could lead to trouble. That trouble, I believe, would come from the wrong kind of reaction by society, *not* from the actions of the young people."

And another parent: "I agree that youth are pushing for *some* needed reforms, most of it to the good. The violence is inexcusable, though I am confident extremes will give way to a forward-moving result. But something basic is changing."

The responses were much the same to a question as to whether the more violent manifestations among the young are symptoms of a degeneration in the moral fiber of our adult society which, if not checked, threatens the survival of our government and society, with agreement to the proposition winning over disagreement by a narrow margin. A professional worker with youth groups felt that our society is threatened, though not holding youth responsible, because "affluence makes possible so many things that were not possible for my depression-age generation." Another comment was: "The moral fiber is about the same as ever; there have always been wild ones who went West. This is an age of mass information and misinformation, instant knowledge of events all over the world. This has created anxiety and hysteria. Those most affected are the intelligent, sensitive young, who are having a harder time than ever was the case before in finding their way from childhood to adulthood."

I must admit that grandparents pulled down the rate of agreement to the statements which referred to shortcomings of our adult society; but they ran neck and neck with the younger people in their replies to a list of eight factors present in our adult society to some degree, of which I asked my adult advisers to indicate the ones they held responsible for the youth unrest and to star any they considered especially at fault. A very great majority expressed agreement with, and many starred, the following: (1) Bad examples set by adults with regard to drinking, sex behavior, marriage breakups, contempt for law, etc. (2) The permissiveness prevailing in much child training and educational theory during the past two decades. (3) Lowering of the general moral climate, as evidenced by the explosion of raw sex in reading matter, movies and theater, violence on TV, malfeasance by public officials and repudiation of obligations, such as illegal strikes by civil service employees engaged in essential services. (4) Frustration and justified resentment by youth over Vietnam and the draft—parents contributing a greater majority and more stars to this one than grandparents and nonparents. And (5) anxiety of middle-class parents to give their offspring "advantages," whether or not they have merited or want them.

Agreement and disagreement were nearly half and half on (6) serious failure of schools and colleges to give the young people what they need, and agreement led by a small margin on

(7) deliberate beaming of advertising at children and teen-agers, though both got a few stars. The only one where dis-agreement won out, and this was by more than two to one, was the breaking down of paternal power through TV serials and movies which represent Dad as a bumbling idiot; a number felt paternal power had declined, but not for the reason stated.

Several accepted my invitation to add to the list of factors in our adult society contributing to unrest in youth, as follows: "The availability of drugs and the establishment of poor moral standards by advertising." "Many good middle-class young people are so criminally ignored—bought off, really—that they have no place to go for guidance." "The mother working, as well as the breakdown of a father as the head of a household, has contributed to the bad state we are in today. Mothers pacify children with material things to make up for the time and attention they should be giving but aren't."

"One of our main faults is that in the upbringing of our children we have not given them the opportunity, or required them, to *give* of themselves. They have been takers rather than givers. In societies where the children are needed in the scheme of survival and contribute their share from early years, rebellion is not common. Also, material things have meant too much in the lives of the present older generation. In the face of world-wide destruction by nuclear devices, pesticides, oxygen exhaus-tion, these things are no longer the goals of the young, hence rebellion against being slotted in the military-industrial setup."

I can think of still more myself, but among us all I believe we have done a thorough-enough job on our reeling, punch-drunk society. The only thing remaining is to try to figure out why and how it has arrived at its present deplorable state. For just about everything appeared to go to pieces around the middle 1960's, taking us ordinary citizens by surprise and leav-ing us as bewildered and groping as youth could possibly be.

Prior to that, we had been making notable progress in two

critical areas, civil rights and the fight on poverty. (As a matter of fact, when President Roosevelt first attacked poverty in the 1930's, he told us that one third of our people were "ill-fed, ill-housed and ill-clothed." By the 1960's, the proportion had shrunk to one fifth of a much larger population, but one fifth was considered a scandal.) I think we have reason to be proud that at the end of World War II, when the United States stood pre-eminent and all-powerful and could have taken over the whole world had she so desired, we retained for ourselves not one inch of conquered territory, nor did we loot the vanquished countries, as has been the custom of victors from time immemorial and was the practice of both Nazis and Russians in World War II. Instead we poured out our own treasure to set the devastated countries on their feet, enemies as well as friends.

What happened to us? My own opinion, from having watched the whole process and having read much about it, is that now we are simply reaping the consequences of a prosperity and technology never known before in the world's history, from which have stemmed overpopulation and the intensification of human frailties and greed.

In an early letter to you, I traced the progress of the sex revolution from its beginnings in World War I. In similar fashion, World War II brought about the great acceleration in technology and prosperity, with its accompanying materialism, to which so many of my young correspondents as well as older ones have called attention.

As I said, our economy never did get back on its own feet after the depression until we began rearming in 1939, and the birth rate and age for marriage stayed within bounds throughout the decade. But after we got into the war, the money supply seemed unlimited, and the needs of mechanized warfare unleashed the full American genius for invention. Technology took a tremendous leap forward, continuing to accelerate after the war was over. There was work for everyone, and for those on the "home front" the war was a bonanza.

One of my young cooperators has questioned the stress I have been placing on prosperity as a cause of our social ills. "What's so bad about having plenty of money?" she wrote me. "I know some rich kids who aren't spoiled or wild, though I guess a good many are. But isn't something else involved here besides money?"

I, too, know wealthy people who have reared wonderful children and who work as hard in community enterprises as they would if food and shelter depended on their efforts. And sons of a number of very wealthy American families have rendered notable public service in this century. But a high degree of maturity is required to keep affluence from ruining those blessed with it, and that's where the human frailty and greed come in.

Dr. David Abrahamson, an authority on violence, attributes our problems to the fact that in the United States there are no artificial barriers to keep people from getting what they want, and the more people get, the more they want.

A Presidential commission found that since 1955 there has been an increase of from 100 to 200 per cent in the crime rate in every highly industrialized country of Western Europe, and states that an industrialized, affluent society increases the incentives for crime. In the United States there has been a 150 per cent increase in shoplifting alone since 1960, much of it by people who can well afford to pay, like the man who stole a $7 pair of gloves and was found to have $600 in his wallet. "Mostly these are just people who want something for nothing," said the security head of a big store. "They let greed take over."

Dr. Kenneth Keniston has attributed youth's dissatisfactions to our society's having succeeded in some ways beyond all expectations. "Student unrest is a reflection not only of the failures but of the extraordinary successes of the liberal-industrial revolution. It therefore occurs in colleges where, according to traditional standards, conditions are best."

One of the young men over twenty, you may remember, in his comment about modern education, said that "the rich abuse it." And, in fact, studies have shown that the campus leaders in violence and vandalism come mainly from privileged homes. Involved in a horrible catastrophe in New York City where three members of a radical student organization were blown up, two of them to bits, and about one million dollars' worth of property was destroyed by bombs intended to blow up other people, were two daughters of wealthy men, one of the fathers being the owner of the $250,000 house which the group was using as a bomb factory.

Technology and prosperity together have taken away nearly all the home tasks youngsters used to perform, in less affluent times, which helped develop responsibility. We are told that because of our affluence and the multitude of things required to keep us happy, the average American consumes or destroys his environment at a rate twenty-five times that of the Indian peasant. And that it is routine for Peace Corps workers, returning home after their tour of duty, to go through a period of deep depression because of the waste and extravagance here.

Our society does need changing in many ways, and you are inheriting the responsibility for making the changes as well as the problems created by the ineptness of us older folk. You need to know the causes of the problems. I can't think that anyone who experienced the Great Depression would really wish its counterpart on our society. But it is your right to know that we cannot get off the technology-prosperity-materialism kick without creating a great deal of hardship for a great many people. One of you has sensed this, a girl in the twenty-and-over group, who gave as the most critical question facing the teen-age girl today, "Raised in a society of material importance along with rejection of the stress placed on material wealth, what does she want? How does she expect to live when she is married?" That is indeed a question for idealistic youth to ponder and plan about.

But in hammering away at the defects of our society, let's not lose sight of the fact that there is another side. Millions upon millions of adult Americans live as soberly and decently as Americans ever did, and the tenor of your over-all responses to my questions indicates that the same thing is true of millions of the young. The people I do business with would far rather be cheated themselves than cheat someone else. A host of legislators have passed countless statutes designed to protect the public from wrong-doers. We have many honest, devoted public officials who work like draft horses to preserve the idealism and generosity America has always stood for. Citizen groups rise up and fight with might and main to save, for your children and grandchildren, the beauties and wonders of the magnificent land left to us by our forefathers, when they are threatened.

Having been young once myself and very concerned about affairs, I know how maddening it is that it takes so long to institute needed reforms. But I'm sure I needn't point out to you that that is the price a large and diverse citizenry pays for the freedom to think one's own thoughts and vote accordingly; instant change can be brought about only in a totalitarian system in which the thinking is done for everyone by a few people at the top, and any who dare to differ are severely punished. Nevertheless, in my lifetime I have seen so many reforms brought about that I have come to feel that if a thing is right in time it will be accepted.

At long last our governments, Federal, state and local, are beginning to move toward cutting down pollution; this will come because it has to come. One of the very encouraging signs is the interest so many young people have been taking in politics, working with citizen reform groups and for candidates who stand for needed changes. The more of you who do this, the more rapidly the changes will come about.

As for the overpopulation threat, what the situation shall be thirty years from now is entirely up to your generation and what you choose to do about sex, morals and marriage. It happens that these very subjects lead the list you have furnished me of questions you consider to be most critical for today's teen-age girls, so I'll take them up next. But before leaving our present society's sins of commission and omission, I'd like to say something about the lack of communication between the younger and older folks, mentioned by so many of you.

You may remember that I asked you if you keep still about your real views on moral and social matters for fear of hurting your parents.

The younger and older males said no, 2 to 1; the younger and older girls said yes, 3 to 1.

I asked my adult cooperators if they hesitated to express their views about sex, ethics, student demonstrations and the like in the presence of the young, lest they be considered square and members of the establishment. Only one marked yes. Many told of fine experiences in bringing up controversial subjects in youth groups or with friends of their children, with the young people most receptive and a discussion ensuing that was profitable to all. I think it is perhaps natural that the girls should be more sensitive on this subject than the boys, since parents tend to exert more supervision over girls and worry more about them. But I wonder if the hesitancy so many of you feel may not be due to an unwarranted fear of being misunderstood or rebuffed, Teen-age girls above all should be able to feel free to take their questions to their parents, and to talk over with them whatever bothers them. Why don't you at least give your adults a try, before putting them down as being rigid and unsympathetic?

This winds up the background of today's dilemma. Please understand that I have only hit the high places; the details could furnish subjects for any number of these and I think would be very much worth researching. No doubt many people would disagree with some of my statements and conclusions; don't hesitate to let me know if you have objections or further questions. And now on to the matters that concern your generation directly!

My thanks to those who have stayed with me through the general discussions.

All the best,
GLADYS SHULTZ

PART II

Sex, Morals,
Marriage, Drugs

What Is the New Morality?

DEAR JANIE AND FRIENDS:

I'm going to make this letter just a report of your responses to my questions concerning your opinions and impressions about morals and sex behavior, and shall start with the one where I asked you to state the three most critical questions facing teen-age girls today, in the order of their importance.

As I said in my last letter, questions concerning sex, morals and marriage led the list. In most cases the answer was simply "love" or "sex," or "love and sex," so I can't be quite sure what was meant.

Where sex was defined, it was as follows:

Teen-Age Girls. All the questions of those under seventeen were as to whether or not virginity has any value. A seventeen-year-old high school senior felt the principal question was, "Should a girl have intercourse with a steady boy friend?"

Girls Twenty and Over. In this group the sex problem was expressed as "knowing where to stop," "whether or not to have premarital sex and who with," "whether or not to engage in sexual intercourse with someone you like but may not marry."

Where love was defined, it was as follows:

Teen-Age Girls. "Will she ever find a man who can give her the kind of love she needs and visualizes?" And the phrase "love and sex," used by many, was enlarged upon by two girls in this group, one expressing it as "learning to love, not just in a sexual relationship but in all types," and by another "as education and career versus marriage—there is no hassle with love versus sex if considered responsibly and thoughtfully by both people."

Where morals were defined, it was as follows:

Teen-Age Girls. Several spoke of the necessity to develop a moral and value system in keeping with a girl's own character, and one gave, as the most critical consideration, "developing her mind to the point where she can know who she is, what she wants out of life and what her values and morals really are."

Girls Twenty and Over. A number of this group stressed the foregoing point, with such definitions as "developing your own set of moral and ethical standards rather than following what the crowd does" and "determining the roles of love, sex and morality for today's generation."

Where marriage was defined:

Teen-Age Girls. The few comments were along the line of "Will she find a compatible lifelong mate with whom she will realize her utmost happiness?"

Girls Twenty and Over. Marriage was mainly mentioned in this group as forcing a decision about the role a girl will play in society—"to be a career girl, or wife and mother, or combine the two." But one states, as a critical question, learning to establish relationships with people "and especially with men, as a way of finding a good husband."

The males twenty and over tended to stress marriage as the most critical question for girls, with subdivisions such as sex and love, one young man giving, as a subdivision, "learning the facts of life soon enough" and another "her attitudes concerning her sex and love life." The rest who listed sex and love did so without explanation, but several included things like "determining a social role in terms of career, marriage and children" and "determining the correct moral and spiritual values for a happy future."

And now at last for your impressions of and comments on the views concerning morals and sex behavior held by your generation. I can see that this will be quite enough for one letter, so I shall reserve marriage for a later one. I am departing from the order of the questions Janie circulated so as to bring together those relating to sex and morals.

You may remember that I submitted to you a number of statements I have heard or read about attitudes of today's young people toward sex and morals. The first one of this group, which I will renumber for purposes of this discussion, was prepared with the help of, and endorsed by, a number of my college consultants, and read as follows:

Statement I. The younger generation has thrown traditional moral concepts and rules governing sex behavior out the window. Nothing is considered wrong as long as individuals don't hurt others, do what they do in private so as not to offend others, and don't cause concern to their friends. (As by getting hung up on drugs or liquor or sex, etc.) Do you believe that most of the people you know would: Agree? Disagree? This was to be answered by checking the little box after "agree" or "disagree."

That there can be a considerable difference between what individuals may think is true of people in general, but not true of themselves and their own associates, became evident immediately. Here are the results and representative comments:

Teen-Age Girls. Agreement with the statement was in a ratio of 4 to 3, with a number stating their belief that it was true in general but not of their own group of friends. A seventeen-year-old high school junior comments, "We have not tried to throw moral concepts out the window. We have tried to make them more suited to *humans* and more realistic. But 'as

long as individuals don't hurt others' is a pretty broad statement. Each of us has his own conscience and a knowledge
of what is right and wrong, and if we do what we feel in our
hearts is right, then we can't be wrong." A seventeen-year-old
high school senior agreed on the basis that "it may be wrong
for me, but who am I to make judgments based on some code
that may be entirely irrelevant?"

Girls Twenty and Over. Agreement won again by a ratio
of 2 to 1, with several stressing the qualifying phrases "don't
hurt others" and "don't cause concern to their friends." While
one who agrees adds, "probably for the wrong reasons."

Teen-Age Boys. Agreement and disagreement were nearly
even, with a very slight edge for agreement. One boy comments, "Most of the people I know would not consider this
right." And another: "When members of the older generation say 'young people,' they should not include them all. Sex,
to me, is something holy and not conceivable without marriage."

Males Twenty and Over. These checked agreement by 3 to
1, with a serviceman commenting that he agrees with the general statement, "but personally I guess I'm not really with it,
for I'm not crazy about the new morality or a lot of the ideas
and ways people express themselves today. I guess the reason is
that I don't want to make a mess of my life and would like my
parents to be proud of me."

Statement II. This was made by a recent graduate at an
alumnae meeting of her college. "It is ridiculous for colleges
to have rules designed to protect the virtue of girl students because most of those entering colleges today will have lost their
virginity while still in high school." Thinking of the girls you
know would you say that this statement probably is: Largely
true? Greatly exaggerated? Untrue?

Teen-Age Girls. "Greatly exaggerated" won by a slight majority, with "largely true" and "untrue" running even, several amending the replies to "halfway between largely true and greatly exaggerated," or "halfway between greatly exaggerated and untrue."

Girls Twenty and Over. "Greatly exaggerated" got a considerable majority, and there were twice as many votes for "untrue" as for "true." (Can it be that the situation has changed so much since they finished high school? The wildfire spread of sex and drugs into the younger grades makes this appear a possibility.) Several of the older girls go on to say that whether or not the statement is exaggerated, most girls lose their virginity in college, and one says that this usually happens in the first semester.

Teen-Age Boys. "Greatly exaggerated" had a very slight lead over "untrue," and only a few votes went to "true," with one responder commenting that "many would lose it in college, with or without rules."

Males Twenty and Over. A considerable majority went to "greatly exaggerated," with "untrue" having twice as many votes as "true." One young man remarked that "a significant number have indeed done so, but I doubt if such is true for the majority." Another young man comments (referring to the young woman who made the original statement), "What a cynic! Instead of Madison Avenue, *Playboy*, etc., pouring out the garbage to titillate the hungry masses, let's have honesty and some frank sex education courses early in school."

Statement III. Boys today do not expect girls to be virgins and don't think the less of them if they aren't. Generally speaking this is true [or] untrue.

Teen-Age Girls. "True" was given a slight edge over "untrue." One girl checked both, commenting, "It depends on the boy."

Girls Twenty and Over. Again the vote was very nearly

even, with a slight edge for "untrue." Representative comments were: "The boys don't expect it but they respect you more if you are" and "It depends on one's age. In college it's true. Boys still feel differently toward a promiscuous girl, but they do accept a temporary affair with one or possibly two."

Teen-Age Boys. "True" got three times as many votes as "untrue." (Again I wonder if this indicates an increase in sex activity at younger ages.) One responder said he doesn't believe that the ideas about virginity are outmoded entirely but that they are changing.

Males Twenty and Over. These responders appeared to be the most conservative of all, as a group, twice as many checking "untrue" as marking "true." A twenty-two-year-old college man, now serving his stint in the armed services in a remote post, said he didn't know, he has been out of the world so long, but expressed a hope that there will be some virgins left when he gets back to civilization.

Subdivisions under Statement III (this was listed as No. 5 on the original list of questions) brought out much greater divisions than the question about virginity. Incidentally, the one, A, was suggested by one of my twenty-and-over male consultants.

A. The foregoing [statement] presumably would apply to girls in general. When it comes to marriage do you think the average man would prefer a virgin or at least a girl who had slept only with him?

Teen-age girls checked "yes" by nearly 5 to 1, girls twenty and over by a little more than 5 to 1, teen-age boys by 4 to 3, and with males twenty and over it was "yes" 2 to 1. The comments on this question came mainly from the feminine contingent. Following are samples:

Teen-Age Girls. "The statement about not expecting virginity is untrue when it comes to marrying time." "It depends on the man. If he is loving, capable ·of giving and sharing, it wouldn't really make any difference. He could accept it as part of what made his wife the person she is, not think any less of her, not get hung up or distrust her. If he is basically an insecure man, he needs the security of being the only one. He probably also would have an ego problem, needing to feel masculine and looked up to."

Girls Twenty and Over. The only comments on this point were by girls who had checked "yes," except for one who checked neither, saying, "He *should* be marrying the girl he loves. My friends would not base a decision to marry on that." Sample comments from those who checked "yes" are: "This does not mean that the girls have to be virgins. But often the guy you sleep with, and who likes you, deep down has a double standard." "I would say yes, in most cases, but I see nothing wrong if it is done as a meaningful expression of love between two consenting people. I think men tend to avoid girls who 'sleep around' as marriage partners."

I may have slipped up in my statement of the next question under the one regarding the value now placed on virginity, for I prefaced a group of questions about sex in dating and premarital affairs as follows: If you agree that the old value placed upon virginity until marriage is outmoded, will you please check the items below which in your opinion fit the new moral code.

The way I put this request may have affected the results, particularly from the males twenty and over, as we shall see a bit later. At any rate, here goes for what my co-operators think is accepted or not accepted in dating.

1. Intercourse should be limited to a steady boy friend wiith whom the girl considers herself to be in love. Yes [or] not necessarily.

With teen-age girls it was "yes" 3 to 1 over "not necessarily;" with girls twenty and over, "yes" nearly 2 to 1 over "not necessarily." Teen-age boys gave "not necessarily" a very narrow margin over "yes," and the same was true of boys twenty and over. One teen-age boy wrote "neither," commenting, "I think the girl should at least be engaged before she ever thinks of it."

2. It is considered all right for a girl to:

a. Have intercourse with any boy she likes well enough to date.

The score here: Both groups of girls voted this one down by 5 to 1; teen-age boys by 2 to 1; males twenty and over broke nearly even between "yes" and "no."

b. Have intercourse on a first date.

The score: Teen-age girls checked "no" by 8 to 1, girls twenty and over by 3 to 1, teen-age boys by 2 to 3, with males twenty and over dividing evenly between "yes" and "no."

c. Initiate intimacies with a new date if he doesn't.

The score: Teen-age girls, "no" 8 to 1; girls twenty and over, "no" 9 to 1; teen-age boys checked "no" 2 to 1, but males twenty and over gave "yes" a very narrow margin over "no."

I was puzzled because the reaction of the males twenty and over was so different from their response to the original statement, that boys today don't think any less of girls who are non-virgin—you may remember that twice as many checked "untrue" for that one as "true." I also was puzzled because a number of the girls failed to check these last items, though some of them made comments such as " I agree with the old values" and "I don't believe in making sex as common as a good-night kiss."

Then I reread my own instructions and realized that I had possibly cut down the number of replies from people who do not agree that "the old value placed upon virginity until marriage is outmoded." However this may be, reactions of males and females and of teen-agers and those twenty and over to the next question in this series were so similar that I shan't distinguish among them except in certain cases.

3. What is the responsibility of the boy if a girl becomes pregnant:

a. As a result of sex relations in a steady love relationship?

Three of the responders, a twenty-two-year-old man, a teen-age boy and a teen-age girl, made an identical suggestion, which I shall give in the words of the boy, a fifteen-year-old high school sophomore. "Before they make love they should discuss the possibility and negotiate a suitable agreement."

For the rest, marriage as the solution led in all categories, in many cases stated just as "marriage," but in a number with qualifications such as "depending on the relationship, and if both the young couple and their parents should accept part of the responsibility." "If both *earnestly* desire it." "They should seriously discuss marriage. If they aren't ready, the girl must face society with a baby in her stomach" (this last from a high school girl).

A number suggested that the boy should marry her if able to and "they feel it is the best way," with about as many suggesting that he marry her or pay for an abortion. One cooperator said, "Marriage if both desire it, otherwise no responsibility."

Since I may, as mentioned previously, have been responsible for inaccurately representing the thinking of young men twenty and over about sex in dating, I shall single out their replies to this one. They suggest marriage in the same proportion as the other groups, and with such qualifications as "if they love each other" and "if she wants it, to provide a name for the child." Several say it is the boy's obligation either to marry the girl or pay for an abortion, one adding, "If the girl wants to have the baby and keep it, or give it out for adoption, it must be a mutual choice," and another, "His responsibility is only legal. However, the boy may and probably will want to marry her."

In fact, the males seem more inclined to legitimatize the baby than the girls do, as a group. There are a number of teen-age and older girls who feel that "marriage isn't always the best answer," that it should be resorted to "only if both are mature enough to cope with it, otherwise financial only," that "the future goal of the boy should determine whether it is to be marriage or an abortion," and "If he doesn't love her enough to marry her, it's much better he didn't." One girl in the twenty-and-over group is emphatic about this. "He should not *have* to marry her but he should take the responsibility in deciding what to do and should share preparations for and expenses of an abortion if that is the solution." Several state merely that the couple should decide together what to do. A teen-age girl remarks, "Feeling a joint responsibility for the new life they have created is desirable and in the steady love relationship is probably there."

The second section to the pregnancy question was: What is the boy's responsibility if a girl becomes pregnant (6) as a result of casual sex, with a girl to whom it was no novelty?

Several teen-age boys still said "marriage," one, a high school junior adding, "It was his mistake!" and several saying that if he doesn't marry the girl he should support the girl and the child, or at least support them until she marries.

The girls are not inclined to be as sympathetic. A few feel the boy should carry some financial responsibility, but a majority believe he is under no obligation to marry the girl and many that he has no responsibility at all. There appears to be a pretty general consensus among the feminine contingent that a girl "who 'sleeps around' and doesn't use a contraceptive is a fool; she deserves the problems caused by pregnancy. Unfortunately, the child does not." And one girl takes the stand that, in this day of available contraceptives, there is no reason why a girl should become pregnant. "If she does it's because she wants a child, consciously or unconsciously; therefore the man has no responsibility." Another suggests that "there is no responsibility ordinarily, but if he ever told her he loved her and knew she *believed* he loved her, he should support her as long as he can," and still another feels that if he cares for the girl he can be of some help, "otherwise it is her problem. He probably doesn't want anything to do with her."

The teen-age boys also declare that in this situation the boy has no responsibility, one of them adding, "The price one pays for being too loose! Most likely, after they make love the boy will never be seen again."

More of the males twenty and over, on the other hand, feel that the boy has some responsibility, but as one states it, "it is less of an imperative than in a love relationship," and another, "Marriage if both desire it, otherwise none." It is suggested that the boy might help with the cost of bearing the child and finding a good home for it, but need give no help toward an abortion, and one young man describes the alternatives as "either an extremely well thought out and safe abortion or a shotgun marriage," considering both alternatives to be dangerous and pathetic. But a fair number indicate, like the majority of the two feminine groups, that the girl who goes in for casual sex must take her chances. "At risk of sounding callous, that's her problem"; "tough luck on the girl—she ought to be taking pills"; "get her an abortion, or if she refuses, let her fend for herself."

It would appear that by no means all of the traditional moral code has been thrown out the window by a goodly proportion of the young generation. This is confirmed by the thumping rejection you have registered to the next statement under the heading of sex.

Statement IV. This was purportedly by a famous anthropologist, who was quoted as saying that what young people today are demanding is legitimization of the things they want to do. "They want the president of the college against which they are demonstrating to come out and march with them. . . . They want the college to say it is okay to use their dormitory rooms for love-making and they want their parents to let them use the playroom." My respondents were asked to indicate whether they considered this statement accurate in general or not true at all. I asked further if this represented their own feeling.

A small minority thought this true of young people in general, but only a handful said it represented their own view, and many repudiated the whole idea in scathing terms. "The author of that statement doesn't try to understand and is no doubt a hard, unreasoning parent." "The above statement hints that in fact young people are irresponsible in their desires. It oversimplifies and ignores reasons for wanting to change things." "No. School is a place to learn. If you want to ——— [sic], go to some drive-in" (this last from a teen-age boy). "No. I, like many of my contemporaries, have only contempt for civil disobedience in any form, and I would prefer a little more discretion on the part of the majority that don't." "No, college or parents should not have to provide the opportunity for lovemaking."

By a similar overwhelming majority you repudiated another suggestion under the same heading, which was: if your answer to the last question was yes, do you think it should be made legitimate for parents also to "make love" with others than their lawful mates openly and under the family roof?

It was made amply clear that, except for the tiniest minority, in your opinion homes are not the place for extramarital sex for either parents or offspring.

The statement did, however, move a number of you to tell me what young people do want. "They are demanding honesty, 'practice what you preach.' They want freedom from restraints so they can find out who they are." "They want to be recognized as thinking, growing, feeling human beings, not just kids who should be seen and not heard." "They just want a chance to be heard and to have some responsibility." "They want their beliefs to be respected and their intelligence to be trusted." "They want the adult world, if it feels strongly about something, to have valid reasons, stick with them and be able to explain why." "They want understanding, they want to find out things and express themselves in their own way, not that of others." "We want to change some things but certain things should stay the same. This love bit is pretty farfetched!" And a male in the twenty-and-over group, one of the minority who believed that the feeling described by the anthropologist was accurate in general though he does not share it, commented, "Students do seek legitimization of things they want, but they also want some of the things denied them by society—they need some new code to follow."

Statement V. The last one in this area, was: Among college girls there is wide use of the "pill" or other contraceptive device. Would you estimate this to be true of: The majority of girls you know, some but not many [or] none.

Teen-Age Girls. Five times more checked "some but not many" than "the majority," but only two girls checked "none," one of these adding, "of the girls that aren't married." A girl who checked "the majority" added that it is true after junior high school of "those who are sleeping with people." Several others qualify "majority" as occurring in the later college years, with one girl remarking, "It is surely not as many as should be, considering the number of those who become pregnant." A nineteen-year-old, a college freshman, checked none of the choices, commenting, "I have no idea. We mind our own business. Of my best friends I don't know which are virgins."

Girls Twenty and Over. Twice as many checked "some but not many" as checked "the majority," but again just two checked "none."

Teen-Age Boys. "The majority" received 3 checks to 2 for

[81]

"some but not many," and "some but not many" was checked three times oftener than "none."

Males Twenty and Over. "Some but not many" was given a slight lead over "the majority," and there was one check for "none." This was contributed by a student in one of the service academies, who remarked that "there are no girls at my school so my contacts are limited. Of the girls I know none use the 'pill,' but I don't believe this to be generally true."

In my next letter I'll start my side of the discussion of the various questions on sex and morals. A million thanks to you all for your frankness, honesty and the concern so many of you have shown.

GLADYS SHULTZ

Premarital Sex —
Yes or No?

DEAR JANIE AND FRIENDS:

I'll try to make my letters shorter, now that we're through with the bulk of the reports and background subjects. Nobody has complained, but I realize that long dissertations are an imposition when people are so busy.

Before beginning the discussion of sex, et al., I want to thank one of my consultants, a girl in the twenty-and-over group, for a suggestion about the letter on society and the young generation. It is that teen centers should work with senior citizen groups on projects for the common good. "There is too much isolation by age groups, which is unnecessary and I feel unhealthy for the whole society, producing a general hardening of the social arteries."

I think that's a wonderful idea. The different generations need each other. We older people tend to become discouraged and overly cautious because we have seen too much, experienced too much; too many worthy measures we struggled for, from the most idealistic motives, have boomeranged. The young, on the other hand, are inclined to be overly adventurous from lack of experience.

Our society in some instances has overreacted to the threat of communism, because so many peoples in different parts of the world had to pay so severe a penalty for our failure to contain fascism in the 1930's, when Hitler, Mussolini and the Japanese war party could have been stopped by determined action on the part of the democracies, while today's young dissidents who adopt Communist leaders as their heroes don't know what we older people know about communism. Working together, we can learn from each other, and the enthusiasm of the young can rekindle the idealism with which we grayheads, too, started out in life.

Turning now to the general statement of the new moral standard with which so many of you agreed, I can see little difference, really, from the one generally accepted by adult society today. Attitudes are much more tolerant and, at least in more sophisticated circles, it is considered that one's sex life is nobody else's business, so long as one doesn't flaunt it in an objectionable manner and doesn't take advantage of the innocent or hurt other people. There is strong condemnation for a mature man or woman who is known to exploit the young of either sex, sexually or otherwise; but where only mature men or women are concerned, who are aware of consequences and capable of handling them, I believe that most people, including myself, feel they have no right to pry into other folks' private lives or dictate to or judge them.

No doubt in smaller places there would be a good deal of talk and possibly social ostracism if a man's car were to stand out all night, night after night, in front of the home of a woman not his wife. I have heard of a freeze-out of a man and woman living together "in sin" in an apartment building largely occupied by families. But I also have known of cases where a man and woman presumably were lovers yet were accepted everywhere, invited out as a couple and entertaining as a couple. There are always likely to be some people, scavengers for juicy sex morsels, who will speculate about relationships such as these, but they no longer have much influence.

The chief difference I see between the new moral code and the old is that, until rather recently, most of those who broke the old one felt they were doing wrong but went ahead anyway. Like a seventeen-year-old girl, seduced and made pregnant by a man in his thirties, who said to me, "I knew I was doing wrong, but I couldn't resist his curly black hair and flashing white teeth!" How many times have I heard that phrase, "I knew I was doing wrong but—" from people who had got themselves into jams through disobeying the old moral code!

I get the impression that, to some of the new thinkers, what was our "right" is their wrong and what was our "wrong" is their right. Not only is the old moral code considered outmoded by these people, but those who uphold it are labeled rigid or hypocritical. That is one reason, I suspect, why older people sometimes hesitate to stand up for what they believe in.

It used to be that an illegitimate pregnancy or birth was if possible concealed—I suppose that was being hypocritical by the new standard. Nowadays illegitimate pregnancies are being triumphantly announced to the world and the expectant unmarried mother praised for her courage and independence. One gathers that it is concealment of an act that is wrong rather than the act itself, no matter what it is, and I am glad a number of you indicate that you do not hold openness to be the sole criterion for right or wrong.

I think very careful consideration should be given to the assumption that "it doesn't matter any more," proclaimed by one highly publicized unmarried mother as justification for becoming pregnant by a man already married to someone else, makes an action right. Isn't it in a class with the "everybody else is getting theirs, why shouldn't I get mine?"

On the matter of its no longer making any difference how a woman comes by her baby, there is some question whether it is in the best interests of the child to be born fatherless. In fact, that is why society placed such a severe stigma on the unmarried mother and her offspring. It was cruelly unjust to the child, who had had no say in the matter. But the racial experience undoubtedly had been that illegitimates had such a thin time of it, and created so much trouble for the community, that strong measures were indicated to keep "bastards" to a minimum. There have been striking exceptions, some of the greats of the world and many very good citizens having been illegitimate. But not all unmarried mothers have the strength of character required to rear a child who never did have a loving, interested father.

I have read that the Swedes, free as they are about sex, are becoming perturbed because one tenth of Swedish babies are now being born to unmarried mothers, many of whom are unmarried by choice. In this country, ethical adoption agencies do not release babies to single women—or to single men either —except under unusual circumstances, it has been so firmly established that children are better off in a home with two parents. You yourselves, through the opinions many of you expressed on the responsibility of the boy in an illicit pregnancy, indicated rather strongly a feeling that, if marriage is out of the question for the parents, it is better that the child should not be born. You might ask yourselves why you feel this way.

I also agree with the girl who mentioned that the phrase "don't hurt others" in my original statement is very broad, and that there can be a considerable difference of opinion between two parties as to what constitutes a hurt, and with the other girls who stressed this phrase and "don't cause concern to their friends." These qualifications, if followed to the letter, could limit one's sex freedom very nearly as much as the old moral standards did. This isn't to say that the old moral standards should not be re-examined in the light of today's situation, to see how many still apply, and I should hope to do some of that. But my generation seems to have caused so much grief through too wholesale a throwing out the window of older values that I hope your generation will be more selective.

Again I agree with the rather sharp distinction most of you have made between premarital sex—which apparently has come to mean sex relations between a couple who love each other, are engaged and plan to marry—and sex relations in casual affairs. There can be no question that there has been an increase in premarital sex. In the middle 1950's I heard a doctor, addressing a medical meeting on the subject of the premarital examination, suggest that his colleagues withhold their advice about the wedding night until they had found out whether the bride was pregnant, since 10 per cent of them were at that time. I just now came upon a report of a study of 1,000 recent weddings, in which it was found that one third of the brides were pregnant. It looks as though a good many are being forced to marry, before they had thought they were ready to.

I have found no data indicating whether the increase in premarital sex has anything to do with the increase of divorce. I have known personally of cases where a marriage broke down under the burden of strain and hardship imposed by premature marriage and parenthood, and there must be many like that. Where pregnancy did not enter the picture, I have known of cases where the husband killed his wife's love by suspecting her of unfaithfulness with any male with whom she had the slightest association because she had yielded to the husband's impassioned pleadings for intercourse before they were married and so, he concluded, would yield to any other man she came in contact with. If a fiancé is overly jealous and possessive, a girl would do well to stay away from premarital sex. But I don't doubt that there have been a great many happy, successful marriages where the couple didn't wait for the ceremony.

The gimmick is that it is all too easy to mistake physical attraction for love, which quite a number of the young now regard as license for intercourse. A woman I know was impressed by the stamina of a fifteen-year-old girl and her fifteen-year-old boy friend, house guests of my friend's fifteen-year-old daughter. "The two of them spent the entire weekend, except when eating or sleeping, stretched out on the sofa in the living room, with the girl on top, clutching the boy in a death grip and kissing him as though the world were going to end in fifteen minutes. I don't see how anybody could have the strength to keep it up the way they did."

The mother was thankful that the couple confined their love-in to the living room, embarrassing though it was for the other people in the household, but thought she ought to point out to her own daughter how tasteless and ill-mannered the behavior of the couple was. "But *Mother*," the daughter protested, "they're engaged! They expect to get married!" Since both were sophomores in high school and slated for college after that, the wedding date seemed pretty remote. Nevertheless it afforded an excuse for love-making of a variety which any adult knows would inevitably lead to intercourse followed by loathing, unless the loathing came first because of the very intensity of the love-making.

I doubt, though, that moderns give much real thought to premarital sex, until they have a young daughter who is deliriously infatuated with a young sprout of whose character the father and mother have no very high opinion. That is the moment of truth for parents.

We were comparing the new attitude toward premarital sex with the old in a group of young people twenty and over the other night and I pointed out that the core of the marriage ceremony, as it seems to me, is that each of the couple solemnly promises, before a duly constituted official of either church or state and in the presence of witnesses, to *stand by* the other, no matter what may happen. Neither can be freed of this obligation without going into court and persuading a judge or jury that the other has been guilty of some dereliction serious enough to justify breaking the bond. (Of course, we all know that people can get divorces on the flimsiest of pretexts today, if they have the money, but it used not to be so easy.)

I went on to tell about husbands and wives I have known who stood by each other through economic disasters, disgrace and long illnesses which made any thought of sex out of the question for years upon years; and how husbands I have known, as well as wives, have considered themselves privileged because they were in a position to give comfort and support in time of need to a beloved partner. I pointed out that to have intercourse without accepting this obligation might be an indication either that the parties are not in a position to carry it out or that they aren't completely sure they want to tie up with each other for life. (In fact, this last point was brought out by one of my young feminine correspondents.)

A young husband, in his senior year of college, told us how he felt about this. "The idea of 'standing by' is important, but it can't be legislated. It is the 'solemn promise' that is important, whether before church or state or between themselves. My wife and I don't consider ourselves married because we went through a legal ceremony, but rather because of the commitment we made to each other. The ceremony was a celebration of the fact that we had already made the commitment. This commitment isn't the same as the engagement, either."

One of the girls then spoke up. "Many of the people I know want to throw out the binding, meaningless ritual and replace it with deep commitment to each other, and shared goals in life, as he said"—indicating the previous speaker—"some to the point where it is not formally celebrated, though the real meaning and deep personal involvement are undoubtedly there and formed by mature, responsible people. They believe more

[89]

in self-control and responsibility and that these cannot be forced from the outside. When this happens and two people are together because of law and purely external factors, the marriage is a lie anyway. Obviously there have to be laws to prevent abuses and crimes, but the structure should be re-evaluated."

I think I understand what these young people mean—that the business of requiring a public avowal, witnesses and a certificate to nail it down implies a lack of trust and a suspicion that the other person might weasel out if there weren't documentary evidence of the commitment they had made. And I am sure that many of the young people who go in for pre-marital sex—I don't mean to imply by this that the couple in question did—are as sincere in intending to stay with and stand by each other as were the people of my day who waited for the ceremony. But I don't think the commitment is any the less sincere because a couple do wait for the ceremony.

The difference, it seems to me, is that in my college days it was considered the decent thing for a man to protect the girl or woman he loved from having to pay a price, which might be a heavy one, for sex relations outside of marriage. For instance, when pregnancy occurs after marriage, there is no problem such as the unmarried are faced with, no painful decisions are required. You have the baby and that's all there is to it. If the husband were to die, the wife would inherit from him automatically—usually one third of a husband's estate, even if he left no will—and the child would be in line to inherit from its paternal grandparents as well, with no need of a legal action to establish paternity. (As late as 1965, in at least one of our states, it wouldn't have done any good to establish the child's paternity, for the law forbade an illegitimate child to inherit from an intestate father, even though his parents had married after he was born.) The child would come into the world with its father's name and would be welcomed from the first as a member in good standing of, and probably especially precious to, its father's family.

If the couple had felt it debased their love to make public acknowledgment of it before having intercourse, the pregnant unmarried widow would have been at the mercy of fate, she and the child dependent on the charity of her family or the young man's family, or, in last resort, of public charity.

It wasn't as though the girls of my generation were not capable of fending for ourselves. The suffrage movement had given great impetus to careers for women, and I have known many who were the principal support of their families when a husband was ill or in financial difficulties, and who were the sole support of children when a husband died. It was just that to refrain from sex before marriage was a manly man's way of demonstrating the love and respect he felt for his sweetheart, strange as this may sound today. One of my college friends, after she was married, asked her husband why he had attempted no undue intimacies during their engagement. "I wanted you to be nice," he replied. "I wanted you to be the mother of my children."

I have run across this theme over and over in literature, that when a man feels this is truly the one and only girl for him, he doesn't want to make her his mistress, he wants her to have the protection afforded by the marriage ceremony before they consummate their love. Even Casanova, who probably holds the world championship as a rake, didn't want to seduce the girl he fell in love with. His long habit of giving full play to his sex desires was finally too much for him, but he really tried for a while.

Actually, the situation of the pregnant unmarried girl is the same today if something should happen to her child's father. Where he is still on the scene, your answers to my questions about illicit pregnancy again make it clear that the girl who is a wife in everything but name is pretty much at the mercy of her lover's inclinations and situation. Unless, of course, she or her parents take him into court and make him pay support, but this is something most people are not inclined to do.

I think it is natural for a generous, warm, idealistic girl or woman to wish to give the man she loves whatever will make him happy. I have known of cases among the older generations where a girl offered herself to her fiancé before he went off to war and he said, "No, I don't want it that way. I don't think it is right for me to tie you down by marriage when there's no telling what will happen, and I don't want to do anything you might regret later on." Rigid? Puritanical? Maybe so. But under the old ethic, it was considered the man's duty to protect the woman he loved from her own impulses if he foresaw that they could lead her into trouble. I'm not claiming that that's better than the newer thinking; I leave that to you people to judge. But I'm personally grateful to have known many fine men who looked at things this way.

There is the further disadvantage of premarital sex that often it must be carried on surreptitiously and under the somewhat unsavory conditions in which surreptitious sex is usually carried on. One of the teen-age boys has mentioned drive-in movies, which have long been notorious as haunts of wilder youths intent on sex for physical pleasure alone. Doesn't it somewhat detract from the beauty and sacredness of sex between two people who love each other to carry it on in such company? This may be my particular hang-up, but it's the way it looks to me.

There is one more thing we ought to consider. People often undergo very considerable changes in personality, character and purpose in life after age eighteen. At my request, a girl and young man in the twenty-and-over group have written down their experiences in this respect.

The girl, a college junior, says: "I was very immature when I entered college. My mother was one of these brisk, capable women who will come into the house, clap her hands and everybody starts moving. I love and admire her, and everything she did was for our welfare, but I was used to having her plan and contrive and had never been forced to do that for myself. In my sophomore year a masterful guy simply took me over. He was as aggressive as I was passive, and as the tail to his comet I got out a great deal more and had a lot of friends and fun without any effort on my part. For a while it seemed to be just the ticket. But then I began to realize that, if I continued that way, I never would know what I was really like or wanted. I began to assert myself, and that was where the romance ended. The boy friend I have now is a strong person too, but he encourages me to develop my individuality. I can see how wrong for me it would have been if I had let the first one run my life."

The young man, who is a graduate student, writes: "I have *indeed* changed a great deal since I was a teen-ager. I will be twenty-five in September. This probably seems ancient to a teen-ager, but nonetheless I feel I've not slowed down as I've grown older; instead I think I have only become more resourceful in my enterprises and use of time. As a teen-ager I seldom thought very much about serious work which *would build a future*. Oh, I did do many community-minded things, church projects, etc. And these were quite enjoyable experiences, just as today's teen-agers seem to find it good to 'help.'

"However, all my play and especially my work (even after graduating from high school) seemed to depend upon my 'wanting' to do my own will. Instead of going on to college I was restless and worked in several jobs. After a year of aimlessness I decided the U.S. Air Force would help the situation, so, on the advice of a friend, I joined for four years. Now the Air Force was 'somethin'' else. I learned that I had to do some things I didn't want to do. This, of course, is called discipline. But at the same time I learned self-discipline. It was a slow

[93]

process, but I grew in both self-discipline and independence, these factors together convincing me that I would not be happy as a career man in the Air Force (independence speaking) and that I needed college (self-discipline).

"Most of the kids at college thought I was a 'brain' because (confession) I didn't study much. The explanation was that I was intense when I did study for short periods and when I really *had* to I dug in. And after the mental cruelty of the scarcity of girls in the Air Force, college was a beautiful place!

"Finally, I think my greatest single change and discovery were when I quit trying to change the world and began instead to try to change myself for the better. It, too, was a long process but I can see positive results. While in the Air Force I was around a lot of different guys and I was in many different countries. I began to realize that so much depends on 'which side of the fence' a person is on. I'm not meek by any means—boy, when I feel the need to speak up I'll do it! But I just think, or rather hope, that I'll be successful in getting myself straightened out before I start in on the world's problems."

I believe we are entitled to deduce from the foregoing that a girl this young man might have committed himself to in the late teens wouldn't have fitted the bill at all after he began to change. I see nothing wrong in getting engaged at younger ages with the understanding that it's subject to termination without animus on either side, and I think that before one marries there can even be a certain advantage in having had several temporary relationships of this kind, on a platonic basis.

But I would hope that a girl would wait until she has had several platonic relationships, is in her twenties and is well aware of the possible pitfalls of premarital sex before even considering it. I have known more than one mature, capable, worldly-wise career woman who had devoted herself wholeheartedly to a man outside of wedlock, believing his assurances that he would marry her if it were not for an old mother he had to care for or a wife who wouldn't give him a divorce, to come close to breakdown when the man, freed of his encumbrance, married someone else. These things happen. I'd rather they didn't happen to loving, generous-hearted, teen-age girls.

In my next letter I'll take up the matters of casual sex and whether virginity has any value any more.

Best to you all,
GLADYS SHULTZ

Has the Male Sex
Changed Its Spots?

DEAR JANIE AND FRIENDS:

A number of authorities have been saying that a society cannot survive without a moral code and that, since our traditional one has been so largely rejected by the young, another must be set up in its place. Judging by the replies you gave to my questions, reported in my next-to-last letter, today's youth tends to believe that it is up to every individual to form his own moral code.

However, on the questions about masculine attitudes and what is considered proper in dating practices, it became apparent that there is a moral code of sorts. You may remember that the girls split fairly evenly on the question as to whether boys any longer expect their sweethearts to be virgins and don't hold it against them if they aren't, but the majority indicated their belief that a man would prefer a virgin bride, or that she should have slept only with him, and overwhelmingly vetoed the propriety of a girl's sleeping with any boy she liked well enough to date, or on a first date, and of initiating intimacies if a date did not.

The males split more evenly on these questions, but as I

said in my letter detailing the returns I can't be sure how fairly those responses represent the feeling of the entire male contingent. Two of the older girls, one a senior, the other a recent college graduate, suggested that teen-age girls should know that men don't hold it against a girl if she has lost her virginity and thought girls should be taught that there is nothing wrong with enjoying sex and they should have no guilt feelings about it.

Certainly it is only fair that men should finally accept that what is sauce for the gander is sauce for the goose. However, I don't take these statements to mean that these girls advocate promiscuity, and it is true that there is no reason to feel guilty about sex engaged in under the proper circumstances—though I can't go all the way with the precept, popular though I know it to be at present with some psychiatrists and psychoanalysts, that one should have no guilt feelings at all, that it is the guilt feelings that do harm.

Guilt feelings about sex desires and about natural and normal manifestations of sex can indeed be harmful. I once had a letter from a thirty-six-year old woman engaged in religious work, who told me she had remained a spinster because she considered herself too vile to be a wife or mother, having done some masturbating when she was a girl. What a pitiful waste! While masturbation is not as universal with girls as it is with boys, it is neither abnormal nor unnatural at certain stages of development, unless indulged in to excess. Then it should be considered a sign of something wrong in the youngster's environment, and it would be a good idea for parents to seek expert help to find out what is wrong, so it can be corrected. Otherwise, it has been recognized ever since I was a young mother that there is no reason to pay it any attention and that it only makes an unhappy child, turning to masturbation for comfort, more unhappy still to issue dire warnings.

A husband, wanting a divorce from his wife, accused her of

being frigid. Her story was, "I enjoyed our sex relations and had an orgasm nearly every time, until he said that he always felt soiled, guilty, afterwards. After that I didn't enjoy it or respond."

I think it was probably cases of this kind the two girls had in mind who would do away with guilt, and I agree with them. Feelings of guilt and worthlessness have been found to be characteristics of many sex offenders, contrary to the popular conception of them. They consider themselves so vile anyway, possibly because of sex play in childhood that was severely punished and represented as forever damning them, that they feel they may as well be hanged for sheep as for lambs.

But to say that there should be no guilt feelings in connection with any type of sex behavior seems to me too broad a statement. Should a young man feel no guilt when he argues and pleads undying love until a virgin has given in, then drops her, hard and cold? Should a girl or woman who schemes to win a man away from a sweetheart or wife who loves him feel no guilt? Should the people who make money out of prostitution feel no guilt? Or take the high school girl who scorns her parents' precepts and guidance and starts into being a new life for which she and the boy involved have no possible way of providing a home and rearing. Her parents are subjected to the humiliation of asking around for a doctor who will perform a reasonably safe abortion or else the baby when born, must be given up for adoption. Shouldn't the girl feel just the tinest bit of remorse?

Rollo Mays says in his very enlightening book, *Love and Will*, that as anxiety and guilt on account of external social forces have decreased, internal anxiety and guilt have increased, and that these may be harder to handle than the external ones. He points out that it was much simpler when all a woman had to consider, if a man wanted her to go to bed with him, was whether or not to observe the moral code. Now the challenge has shifted to whether or not the woman will be able to come up to the man's sexual expectations, "namely her capacity to have the vaunted orgasm," which Dr. May says is supposed to be similar to an epileptic seizure. He tells of women patients who have been afraid to go to bed with men because of doubts of their ability to perform adequately or to have as strong an orgasm with a second husband as a first one, and says that the new inner guilt and anxiety are causing cases of frigidity in women and impotence in men.

A great many of you have indicated that you think some forms of sex activity are ill-advised for a girl, whether or not they are morally wrong, which really amounts to the same thing, in my opinion. For as I have studied the moral codes of many different cultures—and every culture advanced enough to know the connection between intercourse and the appearance on the scene of babies has had a moral code of some kind —it has seemed to me that the wiser lawgivers among the ancients, nearly always priests or kings, based their codes upon observation of what kind of conduct had worked out best for their society.

The moral laws laid down by Moses around 2000 B.C. have appeared to work so well, in terms of the health and progress of societies that have adopted them, that many were still the standard for Western society 4,000 years later, except for a considerable softening of the heavy penalties for things like incest and adultery.

According to the Bible, Moses was reared as a prince of Egypt and was given a royal education by the priests. He was in an unparalleled position to observe the effects on Egyptian society of worship of the many idols in their pantheon, the incest practiced at least by the royal family, and the harshness of the upper classes toward the lower classes and slaves. It is logical to assume that these observations prompted his stress on a single God who was a spirit, the many rules concerned

[99]

with fairness and justice to individuals, and the strictures he placed on certain types of sex behavior. There is one thing that hasn't changed in the last 4,000 years, and that is human nature. Moses evidently knew human nature.

It must be admitted, however, that the Mosaic code has often been more honored in the breach than in the observance. I think that the average American male has seen nothing really wrong in accepting invitations to sex fun if the "easy" girl appealed to him at all. But if he had any respect for his mother or sisters, he wouldn't have taken such a girl to his home. He would have been deeply shamed if his mother or sisters were to make themselves available to other men in the same way the easy girl had made herself available to him. This was the double standard a number of the girls have complained about. Has it really gone out the window? Does it no longer make any difference to a man how many other men a girl has slept with before she met him or how many she sleeps with in addition to sleeping with him?

I will now report your responses to this question I asked you: If girls and women, freed of the risk of an unwanted pregnancy by ever safer and surer contraceptive devices, should claim the same freedom men have traditionally enjoyed in sex, do you think this will make any difference in traditional male attitudes toward women?

Girls under twenty checked "yes" by 3 to 1, and girls twenty and over "yes" by 2½ to 1. With males under twenty it was "yes" 2 to 1, and with males twenty and over "noes" and "yeses" were even, with one male adding, "not very much."

However, the comments show that the tabulations don't tell the whole story, and inasmuch as all the fifteen and sixteen-year-old girls who answered my questions have given "what to do about remaining virgins" as the most critical problem before teen-age girls today, I'll provide a sizable sample of the reasons given for the yes or no in our different groups, just as they come.

Teen-Age Girls. Comments of those who said that there would be a change in male attitudes included: "They will lose their high opinion of women; they would feel hurt." "Men would probably not feel as manly. It would probably cause marital imbalance." "A decline in these feelings is inevitable, but I accept this as part of future living." "Men lose respect for widely free women. They won't feel as protective toward the loose one." "They will respect women more if they have more freedom in sex." "Men will have to give up the double standard. Sex will become less of a frustrating problem." "It is more a woman's nature to love and to have sex only with the man she loves. To go against that nature, even though it is her privilege, might seem to men to be less womanly, less attractive to men." "I think barriers will fall and many more persons will be engaging in sex." "It would disrupt the entire social concept of the inflated male ego. No longer would he be considered the free, strong, virile sex. It will be very interesting." "Most of the boys and men I know believe they are entitled to freedom but don't want their wife or girl friend to be with anyone but themselves. Not true of all, however."

There are lots more, just as fascinating and contradictory, but I must turn now to the comments of girls under twenty who said no. "Of course a man wants a wife whom he will respect to the highest degree, but he also wants a lover who will know how to respond to his sexual 'calls.' The woman must be experienced, and to gain this experience she must have had greater freedom in sexual play in her past. Many marriages break because of the inability to love sexually. If society suppresses the freedom of a man or woman, then the unhappier the marriage. Man must respond to his natural instincts." "Women are generally more emotional and sensitive than men, and no matter what the conditions are, men will feel they need to protect the women." "Even if contraceptives improve, many girls wouldn't want or need them and will still keep their moral values." "At least there *needn't* be any change. Because women are freer in sexual expression doesn't make them more masculine, and men should not feel challenged. The basic premise is that sex must be mutual, not the dominant versus the weak." "I believe men and women have different attitudes toward sex that are inborn, and not readily changed."

Comments of Girls Twenty and Over Who Checked "Yes": "Men will consider women able to take care of themselves. Also, the man who has more than one 'woman' and who doesn't have to worry about responsibility for any one woman will have less protective feeling." "It would make a dog-eat-dog world." "For some reason men don't offer women seats on buses any more. Whenever women have gained equality, they have lost somewhere else." "So far as I am concerned a man still likes a woman if she is naïve about sex. He wants to be the first to show her the meaning of sex." "If women don't deserve respect they shouldn't expect it." "Men will respect and protect women's rights *more* because their responsibility for women will be less. More men will not consider the emotional as much as the physical aspects of sex." "There will be more equality, more silly, frustrating barriers broken down and I think a lot of sexual hang-ups will be destroyed. We will treat each other as people, not as sexes." "Woman would be man's equal in sex rather than his child."

Some Comments by Those Who Checked "No": Although men will always have intercourse with girls who are willing, they will want a respectable girl for their wife. Personal feelings don't change that much." "Most young men I have known have recognized women's rights but also that they are physically weaker." "Just looking at the history of women, they have gotten more and more rights in the past hundred years (voting, employment, etc.,) so as to be virtually equal to men. This hasn't changed their femininity, so why should

[102]

increased sexual freedom alter it? Women are still the ones who carry the babies."

Teen-Age Boys. Those who checked "yes" felt: "All this sex business would then be used for enjoyment. Sex was not intended to be games. It is to be used by husband and wife, not by two strangers." "Women should stay the same. I like them the way they are." "It would kill the challenge." "Men will no doubt take a broader outlook on sex in general and not think of it in terms of love and affection for the girl." "I believe men will think less of women who try to outdo the boss." "Men tend to be less emotional about intercourse than women. Thus sureness of contraception leads to indulgence in intercourse until everyone concerned becomes bored."

The few "noes" were in this vein: "For a male, casual sex is 'sex.'" "A woman is still a woman—the weaker sex."

Males Twenty and Over. **The "*Yeses*"**: "A woman who is not a virgin when first dated will be respected more than formerly. Men will realize that their chances of marrying a virgin will become very rare and they will have to eliminate virginity as a prerequisite to love and marriage." "Most traditional male attitudes are based on chivalric notions which in turn rest on the notion of the female as an exalted, noncarnal princess." "It's happening already. Whether it basically has to do with sex or not is debatable." "I think it will make some difference in the attitudes. A man will not be so apt to express them but they will still be there. To express them too intensely would be to say, to the girl, that he does not sincerely respect her independence and equality." "I think a woman now will forgive her husband for sleeping with other women but the man would think of his wife as a 'slut' if she slept with other men. If women had freedom, the man wouldn't think of her that way."

Again, the males twenty and over who checked "no" for

the most part refrained from commenting. I find in this category only: "I can assume that this attitude depends upon something more than fear of pregnancy," "I think this attitude on a general basis is only a myth anyway," and "Not very much I think."

You can see from the foregoing that while the overall "yeses" very considerably outnumbered the "noes," in some cases the "yeses" were for quite opposite reasons. It would appear to be a matter of "you pay your money and you take your choice."

However, there were two things I was curious about that I didn't include in the questions but put to one of my on-the-scene male advisers who is twenty-two and a senior in college.

The first one was, "How would a modern male feel about a young sister's getting into the sex game?" He gave a self-conscious little laugh—he told me he has a young sister. "If she is grown up he wouldn't consider it any of his business. But he'd want to be pretty careful about a younger one."

The other question concerned an impression I have gained from my reading of popular literature that all a girl needs today to be a tearing success in life is to be a "good lay." I asked my young friend about that and he said "Well if the word gets around that she's a good lay she's had it!"

Other young men whom I have consulted have confirmed that though loss of virginity may not count against a girl with men the way it used to, *being* a virgin is not going to count against her either with a man who loves her. A young husband told me with relish of the way he had to work to get the girl he married to let him kiss her the first time. His wife explained that she had gone to a girls' prep school, and though she had had some dates she had never been "really" kissed.

"We went together for *months*," the husband said. "I would maneuver the conversation around, laying a groundwork, but just before I reached the point, she'd change the subject." His wife giggled. "Then we went on an all-day hike. I wanted to kiss her so bad I could hardly stand it. But it was the same old story. Just as I was opening my mouth for the important question, she'd say, 'Oh, look at that flower over there!' or 'Let's go climb those rocks,' and I'd have to start all over.

"Finally, along in the middle of the afternoon, I was too quick for her and she said I could. But she turned her head at the last second and the kiss landed on her cheek. It was months more before I could get her to open her lips when I kissed her."

He added, thoughtfully, "I have realized that I probably could have slept with some of the girls I dated in high school if I had wanted to. But somehow I never wanted to."

I think those of you who have said that men like a challenge are right. A shy, naïve boy might be flattered to have a girl fall all over him, but I would imagine that with the more experienced ones it would be pretty much a matter of easy come, easy go.

Most of the males in our survey seem to think they have an idea as to which girls in their acquaintance are using the pill. That kind of information does get around, in the past having taken the form of letting one's friends know which girls were likely to "put out."

That lack of sex experience with others than the mate may not necessarily doom a marriage is indicated by a young wife, a virgin as was her husband, who told me about the joy they had had in experimenting and discovering for themselves. "I've found that I'm very sensuous, and I glory in it. When my husband and I can have a few days off and get rested up, it's like our honeymoon all over again."

Which reminds me of a virgin bride of the 1920's who is a grandmother now. A very pretty, popular girl, she had turned down a number of good offers and had waited for a young man who was not yet in a position to support her as he would like to do. "We didn't have relations during our engagement," she said. "We felt that something should be saved for marriage." At last the promotion came that made marriage possible, the couple rented a house in the city where the young man was to head a branch office, furnished it down to the last detail, then got married and drove directly to their new home from the wedding reception.

"We parked and went up the walk as sedately as any old married couple," she told me. "Then as soon as we closed the front door, we *tore* for the bedroom, shedding our clothes as we ran!"

If, as some of my young cooperators suggested, all restraints should be removed from sex activity and the same freedom become socially acceptable for females that has traditionally been enjoyed by males, what would be the effect on our society? I'll go into that in my next letter.

All best,
GLADYS SHULTZ

LETTER 9.

When Sex
Can Be Destructive

DEAR JANIE AND FRIENDS:

I have received a most interesting communication from a young man in the twenty-and-over group who thinks I haven't fully grasped the "new morality." He says: "I think there are two (and maybe more) new moralities. One is the 'new' but actually old morality represented by *Playboy* and other sex merchants. The other is the lovely *true* morality, not in the sense of never having been thought of before but of never having been put into practice in any widespread way. To me *Playboy* represents the old morality merely brought into the open and with a few restrictions removed. *Playboy* doesn't treat women as people but as sex objects, and men are not dealt with any better except that they are the ones to take advantage of the sex objects (women). This is an extension of a double standard which has long existed and still exists in certain cultures such as in Latin America. True, our parents and our grandparents were not necessarily part of this double standard, but the double standard exists. *Playboy* does not deal with mutual respect, real love based on commitment and work together, etc., etc.

"However, the lovely *new* morality is, in effect, to live up to the ideals of honesty, mutual respect, love, etc., with some changes in terms of sex and drugs. But when it comes to sex, *this* morality emphasizes not promiscuity but love and mutual respect. Sex need not be postponed until marriage or limited to one person as long as the relationship has love, mutual respect, consideration for other persons' feelings and desires, honesty, etc. This morality is a highly selective one in terms of a sex partner, although not limited to one person.

"But the new morality is much more than sex and drugs, it is a living up to the ideals of fair dealing with people, peace towards others of different philosophies, rejection of war as a means of solving problems, rejection of racial intolerance. Thus the new morality is a desire to have society live up to what it proclaims to be.

"I have not been very lucid in the above description of the 'new' morality, but I feel it is actually a rejection of the philosophy of *Playboy* in sexual matters. I think you have not really seen what the new morality is to those involved with it but rather the image of it which society holds in an attempt to discredit it. I personally think that in the process of attempting to truly find a new morality or philosophy of life, many young people have made mistakes which advice from adults could help, but that they are sincerely striving for a new philosophy of life because they cannot hold with the hypocritical one their parents have handed them. They are trying to live to the best of their beliefs with the skills they have. They recognize that this country has more freedom and justice than most, but they also recognize that it is not all it proclaims to be or all that it should be."

I'm very grateful for this valuable contribution. Interestingly, another of my young friends had referred me to *Playboy* as representing the moral philosophy of the young generation, and I'd been hoping it isn't so. I also agree wholeheartedly with the emphasis the writer of the foregoing places on such things as love, respect, honesty and dealing fairly.

I have heard psychiatrists, psychologists, sociologists and at least one anthropologist say they think the new openness about sex is wholesome, doing away with harmful sex hang-ups, just as some of you have suggested. But Erik Erikson, in his book *Identity: Youth and Crisis,* says that while symptoms of hysteria grown out of repressed sex wishes have decreased as a result of the new enlightenment, they have been replaced by character problems. "What in Freud's day was a neurotic epidemiology with social implications has, in our time, become a series of social movements with neurotic implications."

That is the way the explosion of pornography, nudity, four-letter words, and exhibitions of every kind of sex activity appears to me. However, I am not prepared to say that a departture from traditional moral standards, by itself, is necessarily ruinous, as long as the practitioners remain vigorous, active in affairs and don't cloud their minds and weaken their bodies with drugs or excess liquor.

If the sex explosion among adults and the sex rebellion of a sector of youth had been accompanied by a great upsurge of the qualities mentioned by my young correspondent at the beginning of this letter, and of others necessary for a good society—honesty, fairness, consideration for others, respect for other people's opinions and rights—I would say, "You have convinced me. The old moral code was a hindrance instead of a help." I need hardly say that such has not been the case. Here are some of the factors in our own society that worry me:

1. The physical deterioration of the American male. James Dickey, the poet-novelist, ascribes this to the abandonment of what he describes as the virtues that made Rome great so long as its citizens practiced them—abstinence, effort, self-discipline—and in our terms might be labeled the Puritan

characteristics which now have fallen into such disrepute. "The whole turn of our culture is to relax, enjoy, indulge. . . . We've thrown our bodies away, comfort has beaten us. The American male has grown soft and the women know it."

2. The public taste for stronger and stronger violence and horror, supplied by movies, TV and reading material. Sex has always been an accompaniment of violence and killing in warfare. Arson is known to have a sexual basis, and some psychiatrists believe that the bombings by young dissidents have sexual overtones, particularly, it seems to me, in the antipersonnel bombs, designed to blow human beings to pieces, found in amateur bomb factories in cases where the would-be blowers-up were instead blown to pieces themselves. Our society isn't as bad as all that, and the Columbia University students for whom allegedly one set of antipersonnel bombs was being prepared certainly had done nothing to merit such savagery.

One of my adult cooperators reports that she lives on the edge of the campus of one of our state universities "in the exact center of hippies, pot, arson, muggings and murder in which this district leads. Four hundred police massed on the campus in one day, a prof friend almost burned alive in her office, profs threatened with steel pipes, and vandalism beyond reckoning. Four bombs exploded within a radius of one block, in one week, spiked with tacks and set to go off at intervals, so that any cop who answered the first blast would get it on the second. The rapes take place practically in public. The university puts a quietus on publicizing these things." No wonder; the parents and taxpayers might get a little restive.

3. The increase in sadism and emphasis on the death theme in pornography and in many so-called respectable novels. The sadist is either an emotionally sick person, or impotent, or one who has exhausted the thrill possibilities of normal and deviant sex activities and turns to cruelty to arouse his sensuality.

4. The growing aggressiveness of "emancipated" women in

sex matters, demanding orgasms as their right and, so I'm told, developing insecurities in men about their ability to come up to expectations. The word "orgasm" was never spoken by my generation in our young days, and well-brought-up girls didn't know there was such a thing until sex inhibitions and frigidity began to be written about in the 1920's. It apparently has become such a part of the modern scene and such a symbol of feminine excellence in the sexual arts that one of the young men, an eighteen-year-old college sophomore, writes, "I could safely say that 90 per cent of the females who have had intercourse either have never had an orgasm at all or only once. Most women fake orgasms for fear of being considered 'frigid.' " The up-to-date woman, on the other hand, blames any shortcoming in this area on her partner.

I have read excerpts from an essay by a member of one of the "liberation for women" groups that have been springing up, in which the writer contends that women are so constructed physiologically that they can't achieve orgasm in normal intercourse—which will be news, I'm sure, to many a woman who loves her husband—and that normal intercourse has been the standard by men for their own selfish benefit. She says that women "must begin to demand that if a certain sexual position or technique now defined as 'standard' is not mutually conducive to orgasm, then it should no longer be defined as standard."

The statement that, because of the way our bodies are constructed, we women can't have orgasms in normal intercourse is untrue, defies logic and is contrary to the experience of millions of normally sexed women.

Certainly the desires of both partners should be consulted, and on occasions where pregnancy is not wanted and contraceptives are not available it is only common sense to be extra careful. But the consideration should be mutual. The hostility toward the opposite sex evidenced by members of our sex who are seeking to free the American female from the "tyranny" of the American male—a laugh if there ever was one—when directed toward turning what should be the ultimate expression of love between a man and a woman into a power struggle, is the poorest possible augury for the happiness of marriages and family life if girls of your generation should follow the lead of these modern-day Amazons.

5. The frightening increase of pregnancies among early teenagers and even younger girls, with twelve- and thirteen-year-olds returning to clinics with second pregnancies. This has reached a point in New York City where the Board of Education issued grade school personnel instructions for delivering a baby. It was explained that so far only one elementary-school girl had had her baby during school hours, but that 900 pregnant girls were attending the elementary schools and it was thought that teachers should be prepared. These children are the least fitted of any members of our society to rear the children they produce to be strong, self-reliant, productive citizens.

6. The—if possibly—even more alarming spread of drugs among the young, which rates a letter all to itself.

7. The growing intransigeance of groups of all kinds, young and older, making unrealistic demands, without regard to what these will do to our society or the institution they are besieging, committing lawless acts and threatening to commit worse ones when their demands are not instantly met. A society cannot exist unless its members are willing to make reasonable concessions to the needs and rights of others.

Not a very cheery note to leave you on, but the trend doesn't have to continue. We'll see in later letters if something can't be done about it.

Thanks again to my young correspondent for his clarification, and best always to you all.

GLADYS SHULTZ

LETTER 10.

Sex in College Dormitories

DEAR JANIE AND FRIENDS:

Let's take a look now at the growing permissiveness of colleges in the matter of sex as well as other types of freedom. You may remember that in the responses to the statement made by a college alumna that most girls lose their virginity in high school, the majority believed this to be greatly exaggerated, with a number checking "entirely untrue," and that several girls in the twenty-and-over group commented that most girls lose their virginity in college, with one stating that they lose it in the first semester.

One girl in the twenty-and-over group commented, "There are many girls who are still virgins when they reach college, and rules are important in the beginning (first year) until a girl is secure enough in her position to make a choice about sex, not to be drawn into a position she doesn't want but needs for security. Rules for freshman girls are important. Guys can be persistent, and many girls don't even know what is going on."

I next asked, "Do you feel that there are other reasons for colleges to abolish rules regarding social behavior? If yes, what are they?"

Quite a number in all the four categories into which I have

grouped my young cooperators expressed the opinion that rules are futile. "If you're going to sleep with someone, there's damn little your parents or college rules can do about it." "Students for the most part ignore them; this creates dissension. Rules of this nature should be abolished or enforced much more vigorously."

Others took the ground that college rules interfere with development of responsibility. "Girls are generally a bit too mature for such formalities. Give them some responsibility and they will be responsible. A curfew never protected anyone's virtue." "I think if a girl is mature enough to go away to school and willing to accept the responsibilities of society, she would be able to decide what's right and wrong." "The more a college lets up on its rules, the more mature she becomes."

A number held the view that "The rules are obsolete in this new generation. Why create a repression or starvation of a truly natural act in human beings?" "I disagree with legislating moral behavior. Civil and college authorities should have no power over actions of this nature." "No one has the right to impose moral restrictions on mature, responsible people. Colleges should help people reach this state, not try to make decisions for them." A teen-age girl says, "Colleges would give better assistance to girls if the adults who considered traditional morals valid would *say why*. In this situation rules per se would be unnecessary."

But there are a greater number who consider rules desirable and do not believe that college is the place for sex activities.

"Whether or not all realize it, it is harder for a girl to look out for herself. The rules should be kept." "Already I am beginning to feel pressures toward a different image than that of a wife and mother." "The rules regulating social behavior should be taught." "There have to be some rules because too many kids can't handle their own affairs, especially in a place completely removed from parents."

Sex in College Dormitories

The feeling that sex should be kept out of college life came through very strongly in the many comments made in disagreeing, by an overwhelming majority, with the statement by the anthropologist that today's young people want legitimization of love-making in college dormitories and home playrooms.

"Sex is a minor issue in college protests. Most center about deeper, more idealistic issues." "I wouldn't want such a place for love-making, if I wanted to make love." "*Some* youths want laxer rules and love-making and the colleges to change their opinion about the pill, but not the majority." "Students don't want rooms for love-making; that is ridiculous. They want the opposite sex to be able to visit and talk with them once in a while." "We *do* want some legitimization, but that is extreme. There must be some restriction." "Freedom should be granted to those who understand fully that they are taking the responsibility for what they do. I do not feel such demands today are joined with that responsibility, generally speaking." "I don't want people just to say okay because of the 'cats' and still leave me feeling I am wrong. That type of action is hypocritical" (this last from a teen-age boy). Still others say, "I don't think kids are all that hung up on love-making." "Love and college should be separate." "Probably true of the demonstrators but not of *all* college kids. College is a place to learn. Planning sex games is for diseased people." "Colleges and homes should not be turned into whore houses."

When a women's college did away with curfew and some other so-called parietal rules, presenting the new dispensation to its alumnae as a fait accompli without having first consulted them, and giving as the reason that parents today do not supervise the activities of their daughters but allow them to take apartments and go on unchaperoned trips to Europe, one alumna commented, "But not *all* parents allow young daughters to set up their own apartments and take unchaperoned trips to Europe."

To find out how other adults feel about the matter, I asked my over-twenty-five group whether they would want to send a seventeen-year-old girl they cared deeply about to a college which is following the trend toward abandoning any pretense of regulating behavior between the sexes.

An overwhelming majority checked "no" for a college which: "Assumes no responsibility for policing student behavior off campus (such as holding a pot-smoking party in a motel, etc.) or for the hour when students shall be in at night." "Allows boys to stay overnight in girls' dormitories and vice versa." (Here I made it clear that I was not referring to the new type of dormitory for both sexes, with separate sleeping quarters, but to overnight stay in the bedrooms of the opposite sex.) "Sanctions off-campus shacking-up of unmarried couples." "Outfits with the kind of contraceptive device considered best suited to her needs, in its medical clinic, any coed who wants one."

A considerable number, however, said they would be willing to send a seventeen-year-old girl to a college which permits some of the foregoing to juniors or seniors but regulates the activities of freshmen and sophomores. Also some, including grandparents, made an exception to the supplying of contraceptives, while saying "no" to all the rest, and several of my "expert" group said "yes" straight down the line, making such comments as that, by the time a daughter had reached college age, they would hope she would have her values so firmly established that she could be trusted to act responsibly.

The nonparent group tended to be somewhat more liberal than the majority of parents and grandparents, the younger ones particularly, a twenty-eight-year-old man, a college teacher, checking "yes" straight down the line. But a twenty-seven-year-old male college teacher checked "no" straight down the line.

According to the vital statistics they furnished and judging by their comments, these adults are not a bunch of old fogies, leftovers from a vanished civilization. Nearly all reported college training and some as many as four years of graduate work. The great majority, including grandparents, are active in business or in one of the professions, and a surprising proportion are engaged in work with youth, either professionally or as volunteers. My chance-thrown net caught many teachers in colleges and high schools, psychologists, a psychiatric social worker, several lawyers, a young minister, members of college boards of trustees and persons engaged with Boy or Girl Scouts, Y.M.C.A., Y.W.C.A. and church groups. They care about youth or they wouldn't have bothered to fill out my questionnaire. They confirm that there are many parents who do not go along with the permissive ones whose example the college in question was following.

It would appear that, in some cases at least, colleges have yielded to demands of small groups of students in order to buy some temporary peace, in precisely the same way that students' parents obviously have given way to tantrums and threats, in the hope that if they go along this time the youngsters will be reasonable henceforward. In such cases, it hasn't appeared to work any better for the colleges than it has for the parents.

Is this attitude being fair to the great number of parents who have carried out their parental duties conscientiously and to the great number of students who don't want the liberties demanded by small groups of dissidents? Is it fair to the dissidents themselves to yield to childish modes of rebellion? I have known grown women who got their way by lying down on the floor and kicking and screaming until a husband couldn't stand it any longer and gave in. But these were not happy, successful women. Only an exceptionally mild and tolerant husband would put up with such tactics, and there are few employers who will.

As to the effect the trend will have on your future society, this is a matter for which the past provides us with no guide-lines. Rack my brains as I will, I can come up with no society, civilized in terms of its own time, whose upper-class families sent young, unmarried daughters to a place where they could acquire experience and adeptness in sex as a way of finishing off their preparation for life.

In ancient times some of the cults which worshiped Astarte or Aphrodite or Venus, three of the various names of the God-dess of Love, had temple prostitutes who were given intensive training in sex techniques so they could provide the ultimate in "venereal" delights to the male worshippers of the goddess. (The word "venereal" comes from Venus and was applied to social diseases because they are transmitted through sexual contact.) But these girls were not daughters of the aristocracy, you may be sure.

In ancient Rome, the highest honor that could come to a woman—and it was confined to members of the aristocracy—was to be a Vestal Virgin. It was a very significant step on Rome's downward path when the Vestals ceased to be virgins.

I have seen Margaret Mead's Samoans cited as examples of a society where sex freedom was absolute, and there have been African tribes which inducted youngsters into sex tech-niques as part of their education. But these societies didn't have schools in our sense, or a written language, and can hardly be considered in the same class with the ancient peoples who built magnificent monuments which endure to this day and left records engraved on stone or written on parchment or papyrus. All the civilized peoples I can think of have set great store on the chastity of unmarried daughters.

It has always been the best people of a community, accord-ing to any standard you may wish to apply—intelligence, edu-cation, culture, birth, character, social and economic status, achievement—who have guarded the virtue of their unmarried daughters; it has been the poorest, the least educated and intelligent, the depraved, who haven't cared. Is it possible that throughout the milleniums, those best fitted to make judgments have been wrong, those least fitted have been right?

One of my young cooperators has said that homes and colleges shouldn't be used as whore houses, which is putting it pretty strongly. But one of the adults reports an experience of her daughter, a student at one of one of the very liberal women's colleges, which disturbed the mother. "My daughter told me that on the first date with a young man who goes to a nearby coeducational college, he started right in to make it a sex party. When she objected, he said, 'Aw, come off it! Everybody knows your college is a brothel and the girls are no better than prostitutes!'"

I, too, find this disturbing, the more so since I have heard similar male comments about other women's colleges. We might ask ourselves, what *is* the difference between a brothel and a college in which intercourse is carried on in college dormitories with the full knowledge and implied sanction of the college authorities?

Obviously, a college girl can choose her partners as a brothel inmate cannot, and she doesn't expect remuneration, at least in cash. But she doesn't need money, because Dad is supporting her. Is it fair to prostitutes, many of whom have little education and no skills through which to earn a living, to be stigmatized, simply because they don't have well-to-do fathers?

Is it fair to the college girls who don't go in for the sex games to be stigmatized by male contemporaries because of the ones who do? Is it fair to the girls who avail themselves of the new freedom, perhaps unaware that they are damaging their own image and that of womanhood in general in the eyes of at least some male contemporaries?

I knew of a girl from a prominent family who was notorious throughout the network of Eastern men's colleges. She was in great demand for gala week ends, but older male students, who knew what she was doing to herself, shook their heads and thought it a great pity.

The new policy is so completely contrary to society's attitudes up to now that it leaves me bewildered. I plead guilty to the charge so many of you have brought, that our society and the parents who have always been considered the good parents have been protective toward the young. At the risk of offending those of you who have told me that teen-agers are grown-ups and should be treated as grown-ups, I have to say that this attitude exists because older people know that even the most intelligent teen-agers are vulnerable in a way that intelligent mature people are not.

That is the reason for the laws which place young offenders in a different category from older ones and for heavily penalizing older persons who take advantage of the young. Society has found it necessary to protect the young from parents who neglect, abuse or exploit them. It is the reason why a man who molests children or uses sexually a girl under a certain age can be sent to prison. It is the reason why parents who care about their young daughters impose some rules in early dating.

The young haven't had the experiences which have impressed upon us older people the dangers of certain kinds of conduct. They are inclined to take long chances for trivial reasons, because they don't truly comprehend that they have only one life and that what has happened to other people can happen to them.

A young girl has a special vulnerability. By the early or middle teens, she usually has become enough of a woman to arouse sex desire in the male, but she lacks the skill the mature woman should have acquired for dealing with tricky situations.

The daughter of careful, loving parents, shielded from rough people and things, can't believe that anyone would harm her. The girl no one has cared about, hungry for a love she has never had, is a prime victim for any male who will put on a show of thinking she's just great.

It is the reason for an unwritten code among mature men who have any pretense of decency against making love to a young girl or taking the virginity of one whom the man has no intention of marrying. They feel that the cards are too much stacked against a girl like that, that it isn't fair to take advantage of innocence or ignorance.

I agree fully with my young cooperators that some parents are overprotective and that girls cannot mature unless given some responsibility for their actions. But I also hold with those who say that this should be a gradual process, based upon the way the girl assumes responsibility, the seriousness of the consequences which could ensue and the girl's ability to handle them.

Here is the way my young helpers answered a question I asked in an attempt to get your opinions about that: "At what age, or grade in school, or stage of maturity (as measured by performance in carrying responsibilities) do you think a girl should be allowed to run her own life without adult interference?" Many gave no specific age, commenting that it depended on the individual and her environment, and there were a number of statements, of which the following are typical:

Teen-Age Boys. "There is no arbitrary time, for some people never mature fully. But I feel that when a girl can be trusted with certain responsibilities and voluntarily takes on responsibilities and can handle them, she should be considered about ready to run her own life but with help from her parents. You always rely on your parents, no matter how old they are, until they are gone."

And a fifteen-year-old high school sophomore says: "In high school there are two kinds of girls: (1) intelligent girls who 'know what's happening' and (2) the not so bright girls who can't recognize a proposition when it's right in front of their noses. This has nothing to do with academic intelligence. Somewhere between fifteen and twenty is when girls should be allowed to run their own lives, depending upon which of the two classes they are in."

Males Twenty and Over. "When she can objectively view the consequences of her actions—be able to make decisions and live with them." "When she is able to support herself or when she leaves home for work or school." "As soon as she ceases to lean on her parents she should be given independence."

One stresses the importance of gradual relaxation of parental regulation. "If parents don't start granting freedoms until a daughter starts demanding freedoms, then 'gradual' will be too slow and the daughter is likely to rebel. The granting of freedoms when girls have whatever degree of responsibility is needed must go on throughout all of early life so that the girl knows she *will* have the rest of the freedoms when she is sufficiently knowledgeable and responsible."

Teen-Age Girls. "No specific age, but when a girl has learned to accept responsibility, disappointments and other realities, she should be put on her own." "When she shows she is responsible enough to handle herself." "A girl should always have a parent's understanding, experience and advice for there are things she will never understand until she has felt or experienced them." "The parents have to be the judges. She should be given gradual freedom and perhaps judged more on how the situation *was* handled than how it *might* be. But when she has left home she is on her own."

"When she can accept the consequences her actions may bring, i.e., when she can pay, literally and completely, for her mistakes, without depending on adults." "Some parents turn their kids loose too soon and they get into trouble."

Girls Twenty and Over. "Whenever she is forced, or given

the opportunity, to live on her own, and profit from or pay for her mistakes." "When she states her readiness or desire to make her own decisions. And at whatever age, as a child, teen-ager or woman, she should be allowed to make her own decisions" (this last from a twenty-year-old high school graduate). "When she is supporting herself or away at college." "It can't be measured by age but rather by experience and upbringing."

When an age or stage of development was specified, the answers ranged anywhere from "upon entering high school," from several of the youngest girls, to age twenty-five, with a number stating "upon graduating from high school," or "upon entering college," or "upon graduating from college." But more people gave eighteen than any other age or stage in development, with such conditions as "if raised with values, beliefs, etc. If she hasn't them by eighteen, she will never attain them." "I do not think she should consider adult advice as interference. I think she still needs it." "If she has good judgment and has gone to her parents for advice prior to reaching eighteen, she will probably be responsible enough to take care of herself and know to ask for guidance."

I myself have always considered eighteen as one of the principal turning points in the development from infancy to maturity. By that time most boys and girls will have attained their full height. Legs, arms, hands, feet and inner organs, which start accelerated growth at different ages have caught up with each other. The greatly increased activity of certain glands, which causes emotional turmoil in many adolescents, has settled down, and the average person has learned quite a lot, though I agree with those of you who have said that after eighteen a girl can still benefit from wise, loving guidance and that there should be no age at which parents should cease to provide assistance if a daughter should truly need it. However, the ages and grades in school furnished on the questionnaires show that many girls are entering college today at seventeen, and some as young as sixteen.

I like the definition given by one of you for a time when a girl should be free to run her life without adult interference as "when she can pay, literally and completely, for her mistakes, without depending on adults." I have seen a report issued by a college which has removed all restrictions that "there is more intercourse, but the girls are handling the consequences very well." But I wonder to what extent they are handling consequences if they involve the necessity of an abortion, as is happening with many college girls today. How many college girls or boys can pay the cost out of their own earnings or savings?

Heretofore, colleges have had the same protective attitude toward the young entrusted to their care as society and good parents, and they have taken their responsibility very seriously. In the late 1940's, for example, a Harvard freshman had to get official permission for his mother to visit him in a dormitory apartment he shared with several other boys. It appeared that too many unnaturally young mothers had been showing up, and one deduced that the college thought freshmen should be shielded from the wiles of women of this type and also that it didn't propose to have sex goings-on in the freshman dormitories.

In the 1950's, twenty or more Yale students were expelled, and their names and home addresses were released to the newspapers, for having indulged in sex games, reportedly not including intercourse, with the fourteen-year-old daughter of a prominent New Haven family who was not named, in accordance with society's custom of protecting those too young to realize fully what they are doing. It seemed rather harsh for the college not only to expel the young men but to send them back to their parents and communities with a brand of shame. To me, it indicated that the college wanted the public to know that it didn't consider that kind of conduct appropriate for Yale men.

The current trend is such a very new thing under the sun and conditions are changing so rapidly that I hesitate to make any predictions as to the outcome. What charges your grandchildren will bring against the society you create is anybody's guess. So I shall just consider some points that have been brought up by my young cooperators and others.

1. Colleges should not feel called upon to assume responsibility for the students' social conduct, because parents no longer exercise authority over young daughters.

The replies of young and older people to my questions indicate that a great many parents, and I would judge the majority of those who send their children to college, do impose some restrictions on social activities of youngsters who aren't fully grownup, and a considerable number of you young people have approved this, as well as feeling that the colleges should have some rules, at least for freshman and maybe sophomore girls. How wise is it for colleges to let the indulgent parents set the standards, turning a deaf ear to the wishes of those parents and young people who feel that college is not the place for sex activities?

2. It is no use to have rules because students will disobey them.

Granted that there is no law or rule which somebody doesn't break, is this a reason to do away with all rules and laws? Is there a car driver alive who hasn't at some time broken some traffic law, by so much as running a red light or a stop sign or parking in a restricted area? Admittedly, continuous patrolling of the highways by police cars doesn't prevent all speeding. But who would dream of suggesting that traffic laws be done away with on this account? Enough people do obey them enough of the time to cut down the number of accidents that would occur if they were suspended, and the body of traffic law is being added to all the time.

3. Rules and curfews have never protected a girl's virtue.

I *know* that curfews and other rules of the past have been a protection to girls who didn't want to lose their virginity to some importunate boy friend. I *know* that petting into the wee hours of the morning has been the downfall of innumerable girls who didn't have to meet a curfew. It would formerly have meant instant expulsion from almost any college if a boy or girl were caught in a compromising situation. This definitely was a deterrent.

A friend of mine was a student at Vassar in the 1920's. One fine spring day she went for a long ride through the Catskills with the young man she later married. The car broke down and it was well into the evening before it was repaired, far too late to get back to Poughkeepsie in time for curfew. The couple hunted up the mayor of the town at his home. Learning of their plight, the mayor and his wife took the girl in for the night, the young man going to a hotel. The mayor furnished the girl with a letter on his official stationery, attesting that she had spent the night under the most respectable auspices. College rules carried that much weight, and no self-respecting girl would have wanted to risk being expelled for moral delinquency.

In Mary McCarthy's book *The Group*, a story of eight girls who were friends in Vassar and continued their association after graduating in the early 1930's, four of the eight engaged eventually in some unorthodox variety of sex activity, but as I remember it all eight were virgins when they graduated.

In the late 1940's, I was involved personally in a mad dash across Boston and environs, through the traffic of a balmy Sunday evening, to get a lovely Wellesley freshman back to her dormitory in time for curfew. When her escort returned to the car after walking her to the door, he reported that a guard was sitting in front of it with a machine gun across his lap! That was of course a joke, but the girl would have been subjected to some kind of disciplinary action, or thought she would have, if she had been late. On this account her date had risked the lives and limbs of four people so that she might get in on time. I *know* that to the male sex, generally speaking, girls are more special when the adults responsible for them act as if they are special.

4. An alumna of one of the free-wheeling institutions discussed the new dispensation with an official of her college. "No one would expect a college to maintain constant surveillance of its student body," she said, "or hold the college responsible for everything students do off campus. But couldn't it have rules banning males from female bedrooms and vice versa, and penalties if students were caught breaking them?" The answer was that the college could, but then "the kids would just go outside. That would be sneaky, which is worse."

Granted that the sex-pots, one hopes, would be moved to transfer their activities elsewhere. But does it make sense to create a bordello atmosphere for the rest of the students in order to save the sex-pots from being sneaky? The last I knew, respectable hotels and motels would not rent a bedroom to a couple they suspected of being unmarried. They didn't want that kind of business, and they didn't want the kind of reputation the places get which permit illicit sex. A man would not take his wife to the latter kind of place if he knew it. Some years ago the American Medical Association held its annual convention in a city which proved not to have enough respectable hotels to accommodate all the visitors. It was considered a good joke that some doctors found they had been assigned to lodgings where streetwalkers took their customers. But no one would have considered it funny if the wife or daughter of a doctor had been assigned to such a place.

I know of a college which in your parents' day left regulation of the students' private lives to a student-faculty committee, all of whom had to stand for election by the student body. After a period of freewheeling, the committee of its own volition set up some rules, including curfews, for it was found that couples wandering around in the wee hours, carrying blankets, were giving the school and coeds a bad reputation which the majority didn't deserve.

Upperclassmen and graduate students should be mature enough to make their own decisions and to assume consequences, but if they opt for premarital or more casual sex, they should not carry it on in college dormitories. Young girls should not be subjected to the pressures some of my young cooperators have reported, and that have been confirmed from other sources. As one says, boys can be very persistent and they are likely to be more persistent if they are able to say, "Everybody's doing it, right in the dormitories, and the college doesn't care, so it must be all right."

Now for the final question: Are those of us old meanies, jealous and resentful of the young, who feel that college campuses are not the place for sex? Should young girls have the same right as grown-ups to get in on this grand and glorious thing? Several of the girls have intimated in their answers to different questions that sex activity is natural and hence desirable, and the young should not be deprived of it, like the girl I quoted earlier in this letter, who asked, "Why create a repression or starvation of a truly natural act in human beings?"

My answer is that when people live in a society with other people, we have to learn to control a great many natural instincts. Also, it happens that human beings are the one group in the animal world who have been given, or have acquired, the ability to control their sex impulses. Persons who can't do this are considered either sick or criminals and are placed in mental institutions or prisons. College campuses are no place for them.

I agree with the teen-age girl who said that those who uphold the old morality should give valid reasons, and here is my reason for wishing and hoping that girls will at least wait until they are out of their teens to make decisions about premarital or illicit sex of any kind.

To me there is nothing lovelier in this world than an unspoiled, healthy, bubbly, teen-age girl, with the bloom and freshness of an innocence that isn't necessarily ignorance but is indicative that a girl hasn't yet rubbed shoulders with the seamy side of life. I have seen teen-age girls lose their glow and freshness, grow quiet, their faces maybe harden and sharpen, after they have entered upon sex. Not that I can spot a non-virgin at a glance—Heaven forbid!—but it has developed that this was the reason for the change.

For illicit sex isn't always the uninterrupted bliss and fulfillment its advocates would make it out to be, and this is especially true for a young girl. Perhaps she yielded in order to hold a boy friend, the reason why many young girls lose their virginity. Having already given all, she has nothing left to give if she sees him slipping away. What will be think of her? Has she lost his respect by yielding?

She keeps an anxious eye on the calendar. If her period is late, she goes through agony, wondering if she is pregnant, and if so, what will she do, how will her boy friend react, what will her parents think, where can she turn for help? It's a maturing experience, no doubt about it, whether or not the girl does become pregnant, but not a method of gaining maturity that those would prefer who care about young girls. And for hundreds of thousands of young girls these days, the apprehension is realized.

My dears, very, very few males who will try to talk a young virgin into having sex relations are worth it. To my way of thinking, feminine youth is too precious to be thrown to the wolves.

Very best again,
GLADYS SHULTZ

[129]

LETTER 11.

Sex and the

Population Explosion

DEAR JANIE AND FRIENDS:

In a previous letter, I expressed my agreement with the statements of two of you that overpopulation is the most critical problem your generation is faced with. This is one evil for which my college generation can't be held responsible. We barely replaced ourselves, averaging two and a half children per couple, the half child being insurance against loss by illness or accident. We were accused by some sociologists, I remember, of not doing our duty by our society.

Again, it was not until around the middle 1960's that the result of failure of succeeding generations to follow our example became glaringly apparent, though a number of experts had been warning about it for decades. In 1939, Dr. Lewis E. Terman, of the Stanford-Binet Intelligence Test and the California genius research, told me of his fear that within a hundred years, the rising tide of the unfit would have swamped the few remaining fit unless something were done to reverse the trend. I took that to mean that it was up to the fit to produce large families, so there would be more to bear the burden, and many of your parents' college generation acted on that theory. But in the middle 1950's, Dr. Ashley Montagu, the well-known anthropologist, told me the situation was becoming so critical that nobody ought to have a large family, and events have proved how right he was.

This brings us into an area where some dearly held traditional concepts must be re-examined. I'll take up first the one which holds that it is the inalienable right of every human being to reproduce as many of his kind as his sexual desires and powers permit, regardless of his ability to feed, clothe, shelter and rear the lives brought into being. The only restriction our society has imposed has been on reproduction outside of marriage, but this is a matter of social disapproval only and our society puts no limits on the *number* of illegitimate children men and women may produce. If the unmarried mother brings charges against the father, he can be ordered to contribute to the support of the child and put in jail if he fails to, but that is the worst that can happen.

I have seen a husky young man, who looked to be in the mid-twenties, brought into family court for failure to keep up support payments for illegitimate offspring by three different women; and a number of men, brought into court by wives for failing to keep up payments ordered by the court, have admitted to having an illegitimate family to which they also contributed nothing. The judge would ask the man if he gave any money to the woman he was living with at the time, and he would answer, with an air of great virtue, "Oh, no, Judge, I never give her a dime!"

In one such case a little woman, who looked like a child herself and whose head barely came up to her husband's shoulder, had brought him into court because of his failure to provide support for his eight legitimate children. He had deserted the wife long enough before this to have had three illegitimate children by another woman, but his wife looked to be around seven months pregnant. The embarrassed judge, trying to find a delicate way to explore the situation, asked the woman, "Well-a, do you—ah—still see your husband?" She drawled, "Ohhh, he comes araound." Only God knows how many children men of this type father in a lifetime, for they scatter their seed as carelessly as dandelions.

I have called this a concept rather than a moral law or rule, because in our culture it is implied rather than stated. Those of you who know your Bible will remember that in Genesis any kind of sex behavior which led to propagation appeared to be all right with Jehovah. The incest that Abraham practiced with his half-sister Sarah and that Lot's daughters engaged in with their father, having first gotten him drunk, did not bring any divine punishment. Neither did Jacob's plural marriages or his begetting of sons on various maid servants—something Abraham also did, both men at the bidding of their wives. However, Sodom and Gomorrah were wiped from the face of the earth because of their immoral practices. What these were is not stated, but we may assume, from the fact that the name "sodomy" has come down for a practice which doesn't lead to reproduction, that it was of that nature. It is judged to have been somewhere around 700 years after this that the Mosaic code imposed the death penalty for incest and for the first time gave maid servants some rights over their own bodies.

In many instances, to propagate has been turned into a duty by leaders who wish to increase through numbers the power of their particular country or religious sect. Among Hindus, poor women whose children are starving or have starved to death have continued to produce another baby every year or so because their religion ordered them to. With other cultures it has been made a duty to one's country. Hitler was rewarding German mothers for having lots of babies at the very time when he was screaming that the German people must have *"Lebensraum! Lebensraum!"*—room to live in—as an excuse for taking over adjoining territories.

Conversely, in our culture practices which do not lead to reproduction, such as homosexual ones, are considered crimes in a number of states, and we have states, some quite advanced ones, which make it a crime for a husband and wife to use certain substitutes for intercourse in the privacy of their bedroom.

The concept of unlimited propagation was all very well when the world was young, there was loads of space, small tribes wanted to build up their strength against enemies, hands were needed to till the soil and tend the flocks, spin the wool and weave it into cloth, and there was also a high mortality rate among babies and children and the life expectancy of adults was very short. But the twentieth century changed all that, as we shall see.

The other factor which comes down to us from early Bible days has been made into a moral law by some religious groups and should be examined very closely, for it has contributed materially to the rising tide of the unfit of which Dr. Terman spoke back in 1939. That is the idea that it is a crime against God for those who engage in intercourse to employ any form of contraception, stemming from the story of Onan which, with its sequel, is told in Genesis, Chapter 38. Since this episode has played a considerable part in bringing about the present dilemma, let's take a look at it.

Judah, one of the sons Jacob had by Leah, himself had three sons, Er, Onan and the youngest, Shelah. Er was struck dead by Jehovah for some offense not stated, without leaving any offspring. Judah ordered the second son, Onan to "go in unto" Tamar, Er's widow, using one of the Biblical phrases for intercourse, "and marry her, and raise up seed to thy brother." The Bible continues: "And Onan knew that the seed [meaning child] should not be his; and it came to pass, when he went in unto his brother's wife, that he spilled it [the seed, or semen] on the ground, lest that he should give seed to his brother. And the thing which he did displeased the Lord: wherefore He slew him also."

It is plain that Onan's crime had been a refusal to provide an heir to his dead brother. His reasons for this are not given. He may have disliked the brother, he may have disliked the widow, or property rights may have been involved. By providing the dead older brother with an heir, he might have been doing children that would be considered his own out of an inheritance.

After Onan died, Judah sent Tamar, the widow, back to her family, advising her not to remarry but to wait until his youngest son, Shelah, got old enough to provide her with a child, and Tamar did as he told her to.

I shall let you read the rest of the story, as told in Genesis, Chapter 38, for yourselves. It is not very uplifting, judged by any modern moral standard, and I have never heard a minister preach a sermon on it. But the widow's determination to have a child by a member of her husband's family, when she could have married someone else, tends to confirm that she had some other motive for her actions than a mere desire for offspring.

I have just reread Genesis. Nowhere else than in Chapter 38 have I found a reference to the rather weird injunction that a younger brother should supply an older one who had died with an heir, which would not be considered the father's own child. Jews have not observed this injunction, nor have Christians. I suspect there would be quite a flurry in any denomination, either Jewish or Christian, which would order its adherents to follow the Bible literally in this.

All primitive peoples have considered a sudden death or a catastrophe to their society to be a punishment inflicted by their god for having displeased him in some way. That a primitive tribesman who lived around 1700 B.C. should have been determining the destinies of millions in the twentieth century boggles the imagination, yet it is fact.

[134]

Sex and the Population Explosion

Of course, the majority of Christian denominations have paid no attention. Nevertheless the anticontraception forces have been powerful enough to make it a crime in some states to give out birth control information or appliances to anyone, no matter of what religious faith. And in states where they are not illegal, birth control clinics have been set up in the face of bitter opposition, with free public clinics forbidden to supply such help.

I am sorry if I offend or distress young people who have been brought up to accept their church's interpretation of the Onan incident. But we can no longer pussyfoot about this. It has resulted in a deliberate withholding from the poor and uneducated the means of keeping their families within manageable limits, means which are available to those able to pay private physicians and to know where to find birth control information. Hence it has come about that those least able to provide for and rear large families are condemned to have as many children as nature sees fit to send along. I once had a tiny cleaning woman, scarcely taller than my stand-up vacuum cleaner. Her husband didn't make enough to keep the family going, so she worked out to supplement his wages. One day she sent a neighbor in her place, and when I asked if she was ill the neighbor said, "The poor little thing is pregnant again. She sure hates it!"

A recent report by Dr. Charles F. Westoff of Princeton sets the number of unwanted children born in the United States as being accountable for 35 to 45 per cent of the population growth. Dr. Westoff believes that the United States might be able substantially to reduce its current rate of population growth simply by eliminating the unwanted births.

It was around the middle 1950's, I believe, that I first began to see references in medical journals to a finding that in some instances injuries suffered by babies and toddlers too young to talk, such as broken bones, concussions and wicked bruises, represented as having been due to accidents, had been inflicted by the parents. Doctors were advised to keep an eye out for this kind of thing.

More penetrating investigation has brought about a new classification in pediatrics, the battered child syndrome, with as many as 900 cases reported in New York State in a single year and one death, of a three-year-old girl, from a beating administered by her stepfather. I know of a case in another state where parents nailed their unwanted babies to the wall and were trying to starve the youngest ones to death when neighbors reported the situation to the police. There must be thousands upon thousands—probably millions—of children who are knocked about and beaten by their parents but not injured to the point where they are brought to the attention of the authorities. Much of our juvenile crime problem stems from children who wouldn't have been born if their parents had known how to prevent it.

It is true that this country as of now is rich enough to feed and clothe and provide shelter and schooling to all, but we don't have the army of experts it would require to offset all the handicaps of being born to parents who are not only poor and uneducated but who regard children as an affliction and treat them that way.

However, unrestricted procreation and withholding birth control information and apparatus are not the only causes of overpopulation. The twentieth century has seen the elimination, through medical advances, of diseases which used to wipe out whole families and either the elimination or amelioration of other diseases which caused child deaths, until today accidents are the leading cause of deaths of children.

In the restructuring of our society along more humane lines that took place in the 1930's, our Federal government assumed the responsibility for supporting children whose fathers, whether legitimate or illegitimate, were not on the scene. There are free medical services and social agencies which help in other ways. While far from perfect, these measures, taken together have kept alive hundreds of thousands of children who would have died prior to 1900 from disease or malnutrition or neglect.

It must be remembered that the span of a generation, set at thirty years, can vary widely, and that a new generation is coming into being every year. Any number of researches have shown that, as a general thing, the less schooling people have the earlier the age at which they begin sex activity and start reproducing and the more children they end up with. So that while my college generation was producing two generations, grade school dropouts may very well have produced three or even four.

A friend of mine taught home economics in an "opportunity" school, for youngsters who were compelled by the law to stay in school until they were sixteen but didn't have the mental capacity for regular schoolwork. The girls in her classes were just waiting out the time until their sixteenth birthday, when they could quit school and have a baby! Nowadays, many girls far under sixteen don't feel obliged to wait till they are old enough to leave school to start having babies.

I had mentioned the low birth rate of my college generation to one of the groups here and was asked what kind of birth control methods we used. There is Onan's method, withdrawal by the male before ejaculating semen, called onanism or coitus interruptus, which undoubtedly has been employed by a great many people since Onan's time without incurring divine wrath; but this calls for self-control and a willingness to sacrifice part of his pleasure on the part of the male, and often on the part of the female. However, it doesn't cost a cent and requires no apparatus. I have read that coitus interruptus was the principal method by which Americans kept the birth rate down so low—the lowest it has ever been—during the depression.

There were douches of acid preparations, used after intercourse to kill the sperm, but they didn't always get every sperm. There was the sheath for the male organ, called a condom, which is fine unless the fabric is faulty and releases the sperm. Pessaries, now called diaphragms, little gadgets which fit over the entrance to the womb and prevent the sperm from getting in, are mentioned in Mary McCarthy's book, *The Group*, as being available in the early 1930's. The diaphragm is inserted before intercourse and removed afterwards. To be effective, however, a diaphragm must be fitted by a physician, and a new one may be needed after a miscarriage or childbirth.

There were suppositories and jellies, containing an antisperm ingredient, to be inserted into the vagina before or after intercourse, and there was also the so-called rhythm method, sanctioned by the Roman Catholic Church, which uses the "safe time," just after and just before a menstrual period, with the couple supposedly abstaining from intercourse during the period of ovulation, when the ovum is passing from the ovary to the uterus through the Fallopian tube, the time when fertilization can take place. However, abstaining also requires self-discipline and will power. Another difficulty is that ovulation may not take place every month exactly on schedule, and the only sign of it is a slight rise in body temperature, which I don't believe was known until fairly recently.

Every one of these methods left some loophole for mischance and required some degree of responsibility or controlling of sex impulses. I know of a member of your generation who is on earth today because his mother, called to the sickbed of her mother in a distant city, left her diaphragm behind. Her stay grew long, her husband got lonesome for her and paid her a surprise visit, without giving her a chance to tell him to bring along her diaphragm. Thus do the best-laid plans of even married couples sometimes go awry, and many and many a pregnancy has occurred because a couple took a chance "just this once."

I have known women to deceive their partners, pretending that they were taking contraceptive measures when they were not.

I believe other factors, added to the birth control measures, enabled my college generation to come up with an average of 2.5 children per couple. For one, up until World War II, there was a strong middle-class tradition that a couple were not considered grown up enough for marriage until the bridegroom was in a position to support his bride and provide her with some kind of home. I have read recently that up to and into the 1920's, twenty-six was the average age for marriage. I would doubt that this would hold true for noncollege people, but it was about right for my college classmates, whose four years in college delayed their entrance into the work force, and I think the majority of us were in our later twenties before we started our families.

Second, among middle-class people it had become not quite respectable to have a bunch of children. Two were ideal, three were acceptable, but those with four or more felt a little apologetic about it, and there were many onlies. I would guess that this was the result of the change from rural to urban living, along with the low salaries young people got in those days when they started out. (When I graduated from college, I had a choice between teaching English in high school for $90 a month or working on a newspaper for $18 a week. I chose the newspaper job, and for years after that a college classmate who was teaching English in high school would insist on picking up the check if we had an ice cream soda together, because of the known poverty of newspaper reporters. Twenty-five dollars a week was considered close to affluence, and raises came slowly.)

That the money angle was important was proved by the fact I have mentioned before that the rate of both marriages and births went down during the depression and didn't start up again until the prosperity that began with World War II.

After the war ended, veterans going to school under the G.I. Bill set the example of married undergraduates, which had been practically unheard of before. I wrote an article about the new phenomenon. It was then that the middle-class tradition requiring a man to be financially independent of parents before marrying broke down. Parents who were planning to underwrite college anyway for a son or daughter didn't see why they should withdraw their support when he or she married.

When parents either couldn't or wouldn't continue their support, a custom grew up of the girl dropping out of college and taking a job to help her husband complete his education. Margaret Mead has said that many of these working wives proceeded to have two or three babies right off the bat as a way of holding on to their better educated mates. It is true that a good many babies were born in the married folks' quarters, but I know that not all of them were planned. In any event, many of your parents' college generation ended up with four or five or even six children as against my college generation's one or two or three. As for the school dropouts, they just went along doing what came naturally as they had always done, and the average age for marriage dropped to below twenty for girls. According to the ad for *Seventeen* magazine mentioned in a previous letter, as I write this the peak marriage age for girls is eighteen.

I have seen some articles which deny the population menace, pointing to the vast open spaces still left in this country, which must indeed impress anyone who flies over it or drives across it from one end to the other, as I have done a number of times. But it isn't just the fact that the great majority of our people now want to live in or near cities, where the big money and job opportunities are, but the way our national resources are being eaten up and destroyed to provide us with the conveniences and luxuries which have brought about what Dr. Herbert Muller of the University of Indiana has called "the highest standard of low living in all history." It's the beautiful canyons flooded and historic mountains mutilated to provide electric power, the forests cut down to make wood pulp for the third-class mail nobody wants and that pollutes the air when we burn it, the pollution of our air and streams by the factories that make the tin cans and bottles and food cartons and wrappings with which some Americans feel it a duty to decorate roadsides and beauty spots if there is no body of water handy to throw them into. It's the depletion of metals to make our myriad gadgets, and the increasing ruin of beaches, marine life and the ocean itself to get oil and gas for our count-less automobiles and other internal combustion engines. I saw a fine three-story house being burned to get it out of the way of a rerouted highway. And in another section bulldozers, clearing the ground for widening a highway, were pushing down a stone wall at the front of a beautiful old mansion with beautifully planted grounds, which evidently had had loving care for generations. Passing by a day or so later, I found that the bulldozers had chewed up the front yard and had about reached the porch. Nothing is sacred if it is in the way of some-thing that will enable the traveling public to get there faster.

Now the experts are telling us that, if anything is to be left for future generations, all couples must limit themselves to two children. Several of my on-the-scene advisers suggest that those who want larger families should adopt orphans or chil-dren whose parents aren't able to give them proper care, as many people have done in the past.

To me, the great threat to your future is the head-on clash between the need to limit families in order that the race may survive, and the obsession so many girls have today for en-tering upon love and sex and marriage at early ages. I've had a note from one of you in the twenty-and-over group in response to my suggestion that girls shouldn't rush into college directly from high school but should wait until they have a clearer idea of what they want from college. She says, "Young people today have a pressing urge to get through it. The men want it behind them in order to have a good start for jobs, the girls because of wanting marriage and being afraid that, if they wait for college, they will miss out on it."

And there's another girl in the twenty-and-over group who feels teen-agers should be taught that guilt feelings are all wrong about "the inevitable natural desire to have intercourse" and that "middle-class teachings about how sex is 'bad,' or not to be done until you are older, spoil the act and make you go crazy, get neurotic, rather than gain the healthy attitude toward sex which sex acts should promote."

That's been the trouble; that's been a major reason for the population explosion. Girls wanting to get married, often just for the sake of being married, without waiting until they are mature enough to perform the duties of wifehood and motherhood easily and well; perhaps neither husband nor wife bothering to learn about birth control or else lacking the responsibility and motivation needed to carry it out on all occasions. So the babies start coming and they keep on coming. I see these girls on the streets of small towns, pushing a carriage with a baby in it, two or three little ones clinging to the mother or running alongside, and maybe another on the way. I think, "Why, oh, why do they do it? Why are they in such a rush? They could have years of fun and freedom and children as well, if they weren't so impatient to assume adult responsibilities, and their marriages would have a much better chance to succeed." With the unmarried it's babies without fathers, whom our society must look after, or abortions, which in most instances parents must pay for, and in many states as I write this a doctor must perform, if one can be found who will consent, at risk of a prison sentence and losing forever his right to practice medicine.

Along in the early 1950's after the trend toward early marriage had become well established, there was almost an epidemic of mental or nervous breakdowns among young mothers. In 1954 I visited the observation ward of a public mental institution during the "social hour," in a room set aside where the patients could gather and smoke, their cigarettes being lighted by nurses because the patients were not allowed to have matches. Except that there were no matches, I could have imagined myself at a meeting of alumnae of a college sorority, since nearly all were young mothers, bright, attractive, many with some college training, and no sign of disorientation or other symptom of mental illness. Nearly all were there because of suicide attempts; one very young, cheerful-appearing mother at somebody's suggestion pulled up her sleeve and showed me her forearm, scarred halfway from wrist to elbow from cuts in repeated attempts to sever a vein or artery.

I was told that so many former students of one of our most prestigious women's colleges had landed in the same private sanitarium that they composed a joint letter to their alma mater on the theme of "you made us what we are today, we hope you're satisfied." I was interested in this because just a few years before I had heard a teacher at this same college comment on the zeal for domesticity the girls had displayed in college, knitting sweaters for their fiancés and champing at the bit until they could become housewives in real earnest; then in a few years complaining that they were tied down to bathing babies and sterilizing bottles and getting three meals a day. This college also reported a drop in interest in studies, since many girls came in order to have a chance at boys in the Ivy League colleges and would drop out of college as soon as they had bagged their man. Nevertheless, the girls held their college responsible when marriage didn't work out according to their dream.

Now it has become a matter not just of individual lives and happiness but of the survival of your world. For it isn't merely the children you and the other members of your generation may have, it's the children *they* may have; and the earlier a generation starts reproducing, the more children you are likely to average per couple. I know people younger than I am, with five or six children, whose children each have five or six children and whose grandchildren have now started into production.

How I wish the young could realize that love and sex and marriage and parenthood are likely to be more rewarding if a girl uses the teen years and early twenties to develop her mind and abilities, thus becoming lovable and attractive to a man with more on the ball than a first or second suitor is likely to have! It isn't that we older people think sex is "bad," but we have seen countless examples of its being bad for girls who start it prematurely.

Recently the mother of two outstanding youngsters spoke of how lucky she was in having such a congenial, happy marriage and home atmosphere, when she looks about her and sees how it is with some other people. I said, "I don't think it was luck." For I knew that this husband and wife were both twenty-six when they married, both had graduated from college and had supported themselves for several years. Both had had several previous romances which hadn't panned out but that had showed them what they didn't want in a mate. They had met through a cultural activity which meant much to both and that they continue to pursue together to their great mutual enjoyment. As they got better acquainted they learned that they had many of the same interests, which they pursue together and in which their children have a part. They were mature and self-disciplined enough to be able to plan the arrival of their children and not have more than they consider desirable.

But how about the greatly improved contraceptives now available? Won't they take care of the situation? Is it necessary any more for people to be mature, self-supporting, self-disciplined, responsible, before enjoying adult prerogatives in sex?

I think that's important enough to warrant a letter all to itself, so I'll say good-by for now.

My very best to all,

GLADYS SHULTZ

Newer Birth Control Methods
and Abortion

DEAR JANIE AND FRIENDS:

Birth control was mentioned by many of you as a subject on which teen-age girls need information. I'll take up some of the other subjects suggested in my next letter, but this seems to be a good time to go into the newer methods of contraception, which weren't available to previous generations.

Actually, aside from the pill, which I'm sure everybody has heard of, as I write this there are only a few real additions to the list I gave in my last letter. One is a soft rubber ring the size of a small doughnut, which is considered an improvement over the diaphragm. It can be inserted into the vagina by the user and replaced every month, until or unless she decides she would like to have a baby. And there is the intrauterine device, called I.U.D. for short, a piece of metal which is inserted into the uterus by a physician and left there. It has been known for a very long time that metal in the birth canal for some reason interferes with fertilization, but this has not been employed very much with humans until recently. Except for the pill, it is considered the most effective device known to date but has the disadvantage of now and then puncturing the wall of the organ or of causing excessive bleeding. Also, in about 10 per cent of cases it slips out, sometimes without the woman's knowing it.

Many of these devices can be bought in drugstores, and some, I am told, have even been sold in certain supermarkets. Nevertheless, the improved ways don't seem to have done younger girls much good, judging by the increase in teen-age pregnancies, and the same thing is true of the pill. As one of my young cooperators has pointed out, the pill supposedly can be bought only with a doctor's prescription, but on the other hand we are given to understand that it is as easy to get as pot. I don't know of any research to determine how many young girls having intercourse have simply failed to take the pill regularly.

Finally, there is sterilization, another measure that is not new but hitherto has been employed for the most part only if another pregnancy would be a threat to a woman's life. It is now being used as a contraceptive measure, and I read that around 100,000 Americans are being voluntarily sterilized each year. This is a simple operation for a man, consisting of cutting the vas deferens, a tube which deposits the semen, after it has been manufactured by the testicles, in an organ called the seminal vesicle, for storage until needed. It does not involve entering the abdomen. In women the abdomen must be entered to cut the Fallopian tubes which carry the ova from the ovaries to the uterus. Sterilization does not interfere with the ability to have an active sex life and is sure-fire when carried out properly, but so far has been a rather desperate last resort for married couples who already have as many children as they feel they can do right by and want to take no chances on having more. Very few doctors would approve it for the young who have no children, unless there were some condition which made it imperative not to have offspring.

You probably know that the pill, the first contraceptive to be taken by mouth, is made up largely of two female hormones, estrogen and progesterone. When a pill is taken every day from the end of one menstrual period to the beginning of the next, the drug suppresses ovulation, the ripening each month by the ovaries of an ovum and injection into the Fallopian tube, where it can become fertilized if a male sperm reaches it in intercourse. When no ovum is produced, there is no possibility of pregnancy. A good many users of the pill have uncomfortable symptoms, such as nausea or irregular bleeding, and it has apparently been established that 3 out of 100,000 users of the pill have died from blood clotting. When this fact was brought forcibly to public attention, several million American women stopped using the pill and a considerable number came down with unwanted pregnancies!

There is also the consideration that while hormonal medication has never been proved to cause cancer, there is evidence that if a woman has a cancer or a tendency toward cancer, estrogen medication can make it worse. The best medical practice has been that when estrogen was prescribed for menopause discomforts, which usually last only a few years, the doctor has had the patient stop the medication now and then for a while. Doctors have been very cautious about prescribing estrogens for menstrual problems of teen-age girls, lest they interfere with the normal development of the reproductive system. One of the doctors who helped develop the pill advises that no one should take it unless a physical examination has shown that she has no condition which might make it dangerous to her and that she should have regular physical examinations while taking it. This is insisted upon by Planned Parenthood clinics.

All the methods except sterilization call for some degree of responsibility in order to carry them out faithfully and the use of self-control if whatever measure one has been relying on is temporarily not available. These qualities would seem to have been in rather short supply in our population since the pros-

[148]

perity that began with World War II appeared to remove the need for exercising them. It is undeniable that a considerable drop in the birth rate could be brought about by making some form of easily applied, sure-fire and physically safe birth control device available to everyone who wants one.

Much research is going on today toward this end along a number of different lines, several with regard to temporary sterilization of the man, as by inserting a thread in the vas deferens, easily removable, instead of cutting the tube. Experiments are going on in chemical products for both sexes which don't interfere with bodily processes as drastically as does the present pill and may work for a month or even a year. Plastic I.U.D.s are available, and one containing copper, which seems to keep a fertilized ovum from becoming implanted in the lining of the uterus and is smaller than the present one, is being tried out. There are in prospect pills for a woman to take if she misses a period, or after she has had intercourse; and safer means of inducing abortion after five months or longer. We are told that at least some of these will probably be available within a few years. But within those few years a great many unwanted babies can come into being who may grow up to be problems your generation will have to deal with.

So what about making abortions available right now, to every pregnant girl or woman who doesn't want her baby? I was very interested to find how many of my young cooperators accept abortion as a fact of modern life, even though as I write this it is illegal in most states unless necessary to save a mother's life. So it is still confined, in most states, to those who can pay the price charged by illegal abortionists and the still higher price when parents who can afford this luxury are able to persuade a reputable doctor that their daughter's mental health requires that she be relieved of bearing her child.

The deep prejudice against abortion, part of the concept

that there should be no interference with reproduction, has also, it has seemed to me, had an element of revenge in it, as though society were saying, "You had intercourse when you didn't want a baby; now you can jolly well take the consequences." The consequences in many cases to society and the new life itself have not been taken into account, and this has been another reason both for the population explosion and the battered child syndrome.

From a purely pragmatic standpoint, I would say that an obvious place to start whittling down the population threat, in addition to making contraceptive measures available to all who want them, is to make it possible for people who don't want babies to dispense with the conceptus, as the beginning life is called. For society's own sake, it must provide abortions, at least until the birth rate has dropped to a point where it is considered desirable to start it going up again.

However, from the individual's standpoint there are drawbacks to abortion. After the third month of pregnancy the risk to the woman is considerable, and the death rate from abortion has always been high, partly because of the unsanitary conditions and lack of medical skill which often mark illegal abortions. But there are drawbacks even when abortions are carried out in hospitals under the best medical auspices, and this is not something a woman should have done very often. I knew a woman who admitted to having had ten abortions. She died at the age of thirty-nine. Besides, a normally constituted woman cannot do away with her baby without experiencing some emotional trauma. I agree with the doctor who said recently that abortion should not be used at a contraceptive.

The laws forbidding abortions are beginning to be struck down, but this will present problems. States which have liberalized their abortion laws have to try to set up safeguards against having their facilities swamped by women from other states. It is foreseen that the free public clinics it will be necessary to set up will have to be staffed to some extent by people without medical degrees. The present death rate from abortions is 100 per 100,000. Only time will tell to what extent liberalizing the laws will bring this down. As for do-it-yourself methods, I shan't go into those; they have brought death to too many girls and women.

So far I have been speaking in general terms. When it comes to providing either contraceptives or abortions routinely to young girls, we inevitably run into a moral problem. I doubt that even the most ardent adult advocate of free sex would extend the privilege down into the junior high and grade schools, unless, of course, the adult stood to make some money out of it.

My adult responders have made it very clear that they don't want *their* young daughters to experiment with sex. In answering a question about sex in the home playroom, as against letting a young daughter expose herself to the danger of a lover's lane, where she might be come upon by police or a rapist, a number said they wouldn't want her to engage in it anywhere, and one father said he would rather see his young daughter dead. Some revealed the agony of choosing between two undesirables by checking both alternatives.

The possibility of an illegitimate pregnancy is not the only fear responsible adults have for the young. During the 1960's there was a steady rise in venereal disease among teen-agers, along with the rise in illicit pregnancies. This is another subject my young cooperators tell me that teen-age girls should know more about.

Syphilis is the most serious one. It starts with a small ulcer, called a chancre, usually in the genital region but not always; then a rash appears on the face or other body parts. If these indications are ignored, there may be no further symptoms for years. Meanwhile the disease is affecting the nervous system and bone structure and may bring about paresis, one of the most horrid forms of insanity, or crippling or blindness or heart disease. The baby of a syphilitic mother may be born with one or all of these conditions.

Formerly syphilis was so dreaded that men have been known to commit suicide when they learned they had incurred it. Fear subsided when penicillin was found to be an effective treatment, and precautions against it grew less. On the theory that the disease was under control, many clinics were closed and the number of case finders, public health personnel who ferreted out victims to get them to have treatment, was greatly cut down. Now the number of victims is going up again, with an estimate of 200,000 new cases each year in New York City alone, many of these being teen-agers. It has been found that the organism causing syphilis in some cases has developed an immunity to penicillin, but no medicine can help if the victim doesn't know that he or she has it and doesn't seek treatment.

The other important one, gonorrhea, causes painful urination and a discharge of pus from the genitals in the male, while the female may have slight symptoms, if any. Sometimes it goes away without leaving serious aftereffects, but the victim should always get medical help for there may be a number of painful complications, including arthritis and heart trouble, and in some cases it becomes chronic. Heretofore the most serious consequence has been that the infection sometimes seals off the tubes in the male or female which convey the sperm or ova to the penis or uterus, making the victim sterile. In the light of the population threat, that might not be considered as tragic as it once was, from society's viewpoint, but might still be considered so by individuals.

Syphilis is spread only through sexual intercourse. The same thing is true of gonorrhea with very rare exceptions, and when I was a young woman both diseases were transmitted by prostitutes, through their customers. Men who patronized prostitutes ran a risk of incurring one or the other, and a husband so infected could pass on his disease to his innocent wife, if he had sex relations with her. This situation provided the theme for several problem novels of the day, the most notable being *The Green Hat,* by Michael Arlen, which was a best seller of the 1920's. Nowadays there are cases where a girl from a respectable home has infected several boy friends. Venereal disease has risen in this country as the old moral standards have fallen more and more into the discard, and the rise has been greatest among teen-agers.

Girls should know that there is a type of malignancy, cancer of the cervix, or neck of the uterus, which occurs mainly in women who have led very active sex lives prior to age twenty. One of the commonest forms of cancer in women, it is seldom if ever seen in the private rooms in hospitals, where the patients are more likely to have waited for maturity to marry and to have exercised self-discipline and restraint in the management of their sex lives; and it is never found in nuns or other women who have remained virgins.

An eminent medical authority first mentioned this phenomenon to me some years ago, saying that cervical cancer was found in the free public wards, the typical patient being a woman who had married at fifteen or sixteen and had had lots of babies. The latest word I have heard, from another eminent medical authority, is that the principal victims are women who became sexually active in the early teens and had many different partners. In either case, it is usually a disease of women who in their teen years had given their "natural instincts" free rein. Cancer of the cervix is one of the most easily detected and curable of the malignancies. Nevertheless many women die of it each year.

These factors are quite aside from the effect on the character, personality and future prospects of a girl who began a sex career at an early age. Some have the strength and intelligence to pull out of it and make something of their lives. But more become dependents on our society through their inability to take care of their children or else, through disillusionment, they turn to drugs or alcohol and eventually take their own lives. I hate to say these gloomy, ominous things, but they are true. If or when contraceptives and abortions should be made available for all who want them, I hope with all my heart that pains will be taken to wean young girls away from a philosophy which holds such a potential for personal disaster.

I wouldn't go so far as to say that everyone necessarily should wait for sex and marriage until age twenty-six. One young man has suggested that my generation was less mature at comparable ages, and I will concede that we were less precocious. In any event, conditions are very different today. We are told that boys and girls are maturing sexually at an earlier age, generally speaking, and wages and salaries are very much higher, though if hard times should come I very much fear that, as in depression days, young people will be the last to be hired and the first to be fired.

But let us suppose now that our government is able to keep unemployment and inflation under control. I know a girl of your generation who refused help from her parents that they couldn't really afford, and has financed her college course herself through earnings and scholarships and other loans. Before she started her senior year, when she was twenty-one, she married a classmate with whom she had been going for three years, who has similarly financed the greater part of his college course. Because of their maturity, self-reliance and work experience, no one could doubt that they would carry out their plans, and there was no earthly reason why they shouldn't carry them out as a married couple.

I can't blame the young generation for thinking the older generations are rigid and biased when they issue doleful warnings. That was exactly the way my generation felt about the apprehensions of our parents when we toppled dearly held concepts of theirs. But it is the reason why I said in a recent letter that the future of your generation and succeeding generations is in your hands when it comes to reversing overpopulation.

How wonderful if those of you who want the earth to remain livable were to get together and set up, yourselves, criteria as to the age or stage of development when the young can begin to fulfill their sexual natures without threatening the survival of all of you. The discussions that would be carried on preparatory to setting up such a standard would draw public attention to the issues and start people thinking about them who haven't really thought about them before.

What I have been saying in these last two letters refers only to sex and marriage. Love in the teen years is a very different matter. I'll have something to say about that in my next letter.

Very, very best,
GLADYS SHULTZ

LETTER 13.

How to Be a
Teen-Age Virgin

DEAR JANIE AND FRIENDS:

Now for the question I asked as to whether there are areas in the field of sex and morals in which not all young girls are fully informed. A great many mentioned contraceptives and venereal disease, which I have already dealt with. A considerable number felt parental sex education has been so faulty that many girls don't know male and female biology, what intercourse is, and a twenty-year-old girl says she knew nothing at all, "not even what a man looks like," until she took a family relations course in twelfth grade, "but I let on as though I knew everything."

To describe these and other elementary sex facts would require a book, and books are available which tell the story. I have written one myself, found in many junior and senior high school libraries, that describes the male and female organs and glands, the feminine menstrual cycle, how intercourse is conducted, signs of pregnancy and how a baby develops and is born, all subjects mentioned by young cooperators. So I shall give a bibliography at the end of this letter and just say here that the very first sign of pregnancy, which I hope girls won't experience in the teens, is a missed period, while a second missed period makes it fairly certain.

The breasts begin to enlarge, the brown circle around each nipple, called an areola, may change color and in many cases there is a feeling of nausea, called morning sickness, upon getting up in the morning. A virgin can be sure these symptoms are not due to pregnancy; if a girl or woman has been having intercourse, whether or not it is pregnancy can be determined in a few minutes by a test a doctor will make. Sometimes girls or women who have been having intercourse and are afraid they will become pregnant may have these symptoms because of their anxiety. In either case a girl should see a doctor and find out what is the matter.

Many speak of the urgent need for better sex education, "beginning at an early age," and for having courses in the schools, at least by high school. It is lamentable that some parents, apparently unaware of today's overemphasis on sex, fight such courses in the schools, thus leaving their youngsters to get incorrect information from their peers, as several point out, or from the most degraded sources. A young man in the twenty-and-older group explodes with "Good God! This generation is as uninformed as the last," and says that what the young are mainly getting about sex is from "the promoters of pornography and from best sellers which exploit it."

One of the twenty-and-over girls urges me to "tell of the respect and love, free of hypocrisy and guilt, many older people feel in connection with sex, the importance of these and why they are important." And a man in the twenty-and-over group observes that young girls "need to know the dependence and trust of a loved one, the responsibility that goes along with sex as well as with marriage." I have tried to convey something of this in my previous letters. And there is the twenty-one-year-old girl who says, "The beauty of sex has to be restored, the beauty of an intimate, lasting love relationship. I'm sure girls

[157]

know of the actual function of sex, what to do, how to do it, but I don't believe they know the feelings they should have, mental and emotional." A teen-age girl believes her contemporaries need to know how and why it is that "males can have intercourse with a number of girls with whom they have no relationship and for whom they have no feelings."

My own contacts with the young lead me to think that the last two areas named, as well as information about their own sex natures and "how you can tell when a boy is getting passionate" are things a great many teen-age girls need to know more about. Inasmuch as every one of the fifteen- and sixteen-year-old girls in our project and several of the seventeen-year-olds gave questions about virginity as the most critical before girls today—"Does it exist any more, and if so, is it a hang-up?" "Is there any point in it?" "How do you stay a virgin if you want to?"—I shall devote this letter to information designed to enable a girl to remain a virgin through the teen years. I think you are aware by this time that not only do I believe this is best for individual girls, but that it is the wisest approach toward cutting down the birth rate in your generation.

I shan't go into the various intercourse techniques. It is perfectly proper for a couple approaching marriage to consult one of the easily obtainable marriage manuals, like the Johnson and Masters work cited by several. Though in the final analysis, true and lasting marital happiness depends upon the characters of the couple, their capacity for loving warmly and generously and their desire to give pleasure to their mate in this as in other aspects of life. But I believe it is a protection to a young virgin not to be all-knowing in the details of sex. I asked several of my twenty-and-over masculine consultants about this and they agreed. One says, "An innocent girl, or one that acts that way, has the best chance of keeping her virginity. Because a guy doesn't want to offend this type of girl and won't make the kind of advances that he would with a girl who seems to

[158]

know it all. He feels the second type of girl must already have had intercourse with someone else and if he doesn't conquer her there must be something wrong with him, so he'll try until he succeeds."

Let's go back now to an idea several of my young cooperators expressed in one connection or another, that sex is a natural instinct, hence to suppress it is unwholesome and does all kinds of bad things to you. They are right about the natural instinct part; but we also go against nature when we sit politely around a dinner table, waiting to be served, instead of grabbing the roast and running off with it, showing our teeth and snarling. The fact is that adolescence itself is against nature, and the adolescent period has been in existence generally speaking for only a few generations since the industrial revolution and the new technology made long preparation a requirement for the complicated and demanding adult life they have produced. Those who deny themselves this preparation have very dim prospects today.

Nature had only one object in endowing the many different species with sex instincts and an apparatus for reproduction, and that was the continuation of the particular species. What happened to individuals in consequence was no concern of hers. You probably know that there are insect species where the male dies as soon as it has impregnated the female, and there is a spider species of which the female eats the male as soon as he has impregnated her. The females in these cases produce a fantastic number of offspring from one impregnation so there is no point in keeping the males around after they have fulfilled their only reason for existing.

Nature has placed in the ovaries of every normal female baby of our species the capacity for developing around 400 ova, any one of which could become a human being, even though no woman could possibly bear anything like that number of children during her reproductive lifetime. There are several million spermatazoa in every ejaculation of semen by a normal, vigorous male, though only one is needed to fertilize an ovum.

There can be no doubt that human societies and morals have been greatly influenced by the fact that the human infant requires care for so many years before becoming able to look after itself; and at a time when predators abounded, a female needed assistance if any of her brood were to survive to a point where they could reproduce their kind. It has been conjectured that this is the reason why human females are not subject to periods of heat like other mammalian females—dogs and cats, to name two—which are compelled by their natures to submit to the first male that happens along. One might speculate that at a very early stage of human development it was found that chances for the survival of progeny were best if the female were able to choose their father from males who offered themselves; and that gradually the family system arose, with the male remaining on the scene to protect and help.

According to the Kinsey studies, males reach their peak of sex urges soon after sexual maturation. They have always been considered more expendable than females—and still are, for that matter—taking on the dangerous jobs and shielding females because the females bring new lives into being. It was therefore desirable for males to have a strong sex drive and to be able to impregnate a great many females when they matured sexually, which in a primitive state was at about the time when a youngster could manage on his own.

Females, on the other hand, also according to the Kinsey studies, do not ordinarily arrive at their peak for sexual response until they are in the late twenties. It is difficult to get exact information about this, for women of my generation were not given to exchanging details of marital relations and orgasms over the midmorning coffee cups. However, happily married friends now and then have dropped hints which confirm the Kinsey thesis.

A teacher of mine later married and eventually joined an adolescent-study group of fortyish mothers. She told me, laughing, of the way her group had embarrassed a young male lecturer when he informed them that, with middle age, interest in the sex side of marriage declines. "We exclaimed with one voice, 'It isn't so; sex gets better and better!' The young man looked as though he wanted to go through the floor."

From a purely natural standpoint, then, it would be the instinct of virile youths to impregnate every female within range, and it is well for our sex that through the ages men have been taught to keep this instinct in check. But it is the reason why men can have intercourse with women who mean nothing to them, and who do not consider their womanhood to be worth very much; while the normally sexed and emotionally adjusted woman has either been given or has acquired an instinct to save herself for a mate who will cherish her and who will love and protect the children she will bear him.

As though to make this easier, nature has arranged a relief mechanism, when sex tensions get too strong. In the male it is "wet dreams," an emission of semen during sleep. The female may have an orgasm in her sleep. Young males, because of their very strong sex urges, often resort to masturbation, and the same thing is true to a lesser degree of females. I know of no modern medical authority who condemns this practice, unless it is carried to a harmful excess.

To this day, virile males can be aroused by many different stimuli—pictures, reading matter, the sight of a female breast when a woman in a low-necked dress leans forward, or of a feminine posterior in skin-tight pants if the lady bends way down. He can be roused by close contact with almost any female who isn't actually loathsome. But nature or something, has arranged that, with normal human females, passion shall develop slowly, with various stages where one can say no if one doesn't want to go all the way.

I agree with those of you who think the young have been sold a lot of hogwash by writers and by movies in which the female star begins to gasp and sigh with passion at the first touch of male hands or lips. It doesn't happen that way unless women are either highly experienced or nymphomaniacs or have already established a strong sex relationship with the particular man, and it is still less likely to happen with inexperienced girls. I would guess that the young man who stated his belief that 90 per cent of females who have intercourse don't experience orgasm was right when it comes to young girls, though not when it comes to mature women, if the male is mature and experienced enough to know how to arouse his partner's passions and to control his ejaculation until she has reached orgasm.

Females can build up their sex appetites by reading and dwelling a great deal on sex. A woman once told me she had read that married couples have intercourse every night. She and her husband didn't, so she spoke to him about it. "Honey," he said, "I work hard, I'm tired at night. But if that's what you want—" It didn't take the wife very long to find that she didn't want it, and the thought would never have entered her mind if she hadn't seen it in print.

We are told that there are very young girls, in the earliest teens or even younger, the "nymphets" described by Vladimir Nabokov in his book *Lolita*, who behave toward males in a seductive way and are a menace, since a man who falls for their enticements can land in prison. But I think these girls are impelled by ideas they get from reading or movies or companions rather than by instinct.

The way passion is aroused in the female, under normal circumstances, is through caressing or manipulation of her erogenous zones, still another subject in which it has been suggested that girls need information. In both sexes, the lips and tongue and mouth interior are highly sensitive and the genital regions more so, with pleasurable sensations becoming stronger the closer one gets to the penis or the vulva, as the outer part of the female reproductive tract is called. In the female the breasts and nipples are ordinarily quite responsive to male caresses, the reason why in my young days a girl's bosom, as well as the entire territory below the waist, supposedly was barred to any male hands except those of a husband.

I am glad one of my girl cooperators has suggested that I say something about the difference between necking—we called it spooning—and petting, for this is the very crux of the matter. Not only was petting strictly forbidden prior to World War I, many of my generation didn't know how to kiss, in the modern sense! It wasn't until the 1920's that the movies raised this to a high erotic art, teaching young America the deep, open-mouthed, lingering, voracious kisses, as though the pair were trying to eat each other, that I see in the movies today and that are calculated to rouse passion from the very first contact and lead the pair to bed down together in almost no time, something that would have been unthinkable for a nice girl of my generation. In fact, one of the first acts of the movie czar appointed in the 1920's was to put a time limit on movie kisses and ban displays of passion. The little smacks that properly-brought-up engaged couples exchanged before the sex revolution began in the 1920's were the kind you would give and get from your father or brother. Because of this and the policy of hands off all intimate areas, engaged couples could neck happily by the hour without getting carried away. I can't help thinking that when the first kisses became a kind of thrill-seeking assault, much of the sweetness and tenderness and pure affection that should be part of new, young love were lost.

Please understand that when people are married, it is right and proper that, in advance of intercourse, they should abandon themselves wholly to caresses and manipulations which evoke passion and are pleasing to both, for this enables the wife to realize her sex nature to the full and in this way make the experience more pleasurable for her husband.

By the same token, it is precisely the kind of thing the teen-age virgin shouldn't get into. For male passions are quickly aroused by deep, probing kisses; it is a male's nature for the hands then to go to the girl's breasts and, if not stopped, on to still more intimate areas, as his reproductive apparatus begins to respond.

You probably know that the male penis ordinarily is limp, being made up largely of soft, spongy tissue, which is equipped with many blood vessels. As passion begins to rise, blood fills these vessels, causing the penis to stiffen, a phenomenon called an erection, so that it will be able to penetrate the vagina. Any but the coarsest male will conceal an erection from a female he hasn't already slept with, but there are other symptoms which I believe would make the most innocent girl aware that something is going on. His face flushes, his speech thickens, his caresses are likely suddenly to get much more intense. That's the time to call a halt, if a girl has permitted the sexy kisses, even though she is unaffected, and all the more so if she is beginning to be affected herself.

Though passion normally develops more slowly in the female, it develops in much the same way as in the male. She may feel her cheeks flushing, her mind gets foggy, she may have a sudden impulse to grab the boy in a tight embrace and intensify the kisses. As she becomes more excited, changes will take place in her reproductive system similar to those in the male. The vulva, like the penis, is equipped with many blood vessels, and with passion the blood surges into them, causing the lips of the vulva to swell. From little glands in the vulva a liquid is excreted which makes manipulation of the organ much more exciting and pleasurable and eases penetration of the vagina by the penis. The nipples stand erect, and so does a little organ called the clitoris which is just above the entrance to the vagina and resembles a miniature penis, in that it has the same ability to stiffen and to produce highly pleasurable sensations when manipulated.

Meanwhile the evidences of passion the female is exhibiting are further exciting the male, and passion builds up in both until finally the desire to have the penis enter the vagina can become overwhelming. This is the way many a couple who hadn't intended to go as far as intercourse can be swept into it without the girl's "knowing what has happened," as several of my young cooperators have expressed it.

Just one word more about orgasms, a subject on which there seems to be a good deal of misapprehension. In a novel I read not long ago, one of the characters remarked that "after all, it is only friction." Not very romantic, but quite close to the mark, for it is the rubbing of the penis against the sensitive living of the vagina which produces the explosion of feeling, leading to the ejaculation of semen by the male and the emission of a colorless liquid by the female organs, that is called an orgasm. The first orgasms of a female are usually quite fleeting, and she may not experience them very often. Orgasms build up and become powerful as a female matures and she and her mate find the procedures and rhythm that evoke her greatest capability for response. This is not as likely to happen in the circumstances under which illicit sex is usually conducted. But her passions may be aroused under such conditions.

One of the young men twenty and over says, "If a girl loves a guy or thinks she does she might, under the influence of passion, be talked into doing it; or she might go along in order not to hurt the guy's feelings. This wouldn't happen if she didn't get into a situation where petting could start. I have a feeling that liking leads to kissing, kissing turns into petting and petting turns into you know what. The smart girl, who doesn't want to be had, will set limits on kissing. When the guy gets too heavy with that, she will go get a drink of water or do something else to change the atmosphere. I have a friend who used to say, if you'll pardon a bit of gutter talk, that there is a key to every girl's vagina. For some the key is petting; for smart girls it's marriage."

So Rule 1 for keeping one's virginity is no petting, and, as the young man I have just quoted advises, to stay out of situations where petting might start, such as parking on a dark roadside.

Rule 2 is not to grant kisses indiscriminately, since so many young fellows today regard these as the opening wedge to petting. Do you remember the young wife I spoke of in a previous letter, who staved off the first kiss for months? By that time she was assured that her boy friend was interested in her as a person, not just as a sex object, and the kiss was important to him because he knew it meant something special to her.

Rule 3 is watch your language! All of the young men I have consulted about this agreed it is important. Says one, "Yes! Boys will respect girls who respect themselves." Says another, "I believe the ease with which young people get out of jams these days doesn't teach them what is right and wrong but only that they can get away with things they shouldn't. Cars, drive-ins and loose talk make it worse. The talk I'm referring to is the common barroom language and four-letter words so many people are going in for. Girls who aren't offended by that kind of language or who use it themselves give guys the idea they are open for anything."

Rule 4 is not to give your affection to a boy or man on faith alone, without his ever having demonstrated qualities of reliability, responsibility, truthfulness, regard for the rights of others and concern for the feelings of others which determine trustworthiness. A tip-off is the way a date or boy friend deals with other people. If he behaves treacherously or dishonestly or irresponsibly or with deliberate cruelty toward someone else, you should realize that in all probability he will behave in the same way toward you.

The really burning question, however, was stated by a teenage boy—how to remain a virgin without being priggish and scaring away boy friends? One of the girls in the twenty-and-over group feels that in early dating years it should be a matter of the girl and her parents "working together to make the teens a happy period, relatively free of serious problems." Parents who back up a daughter in her natural desire to have friends, a good time and a social life which includes both sexes demonstrate that they have her best interests in mind when they impose some restrictions, such as an hour to get home, requiring that a date shall call for the daughter, meet the parents and discuss his plans for the evening, or whatever else seems to be indicated. It should be understood that restrictions will depend on circumstances and will be gradually removed as the girl learns her way about.

A nineteen-year-old daughter of highly religious and moral parents remarked that, rather surprisingly, they had imposed hardly any restrictions on her early dating. She then recalled that her dates were with boys she and her parents had known all their lives and whose background was similar to hers. Her parents knew that these boys would look after her as carefully as brothers would. But in a community where drugs or alcohol and sex ride high, parents would need to be much more careful and particular.

Parental concern for young girls does *not* scare away boys. On the contrary I have seen them practically sweat blood to get their girl home at the appointed time under penalty of not being allowed to take her out again if they didn't.

When a girl goes away to college and is on her own, one of the young men twenty and over suggests that she plan "unsexy" good times with her casual dates, things that will keep them out among people and not allow opportunities for long

[167]

kissing sessions. A girl can always plead a need to study for next day's classes. Warm thanks at the door of the dorm for a lovely time and a sisterly kiss if you really like the guy should take care of the matter. This adviser says, "The guys get the idea, and think that if they were to try something they would be repulsed, so they're not so likely to try something."

As for acquiring boy friends in the first place, I suggest Alice's method. Her family had moved to a new city, where they knew no one, at the beginning of her last year of high school. Alice had felt keenly the separation from old friends and in her unhappiness made few friends and declined the few invitations she received from boys in the new school. Before starting to college the next fall, she decided it was time for a change.

She told her mother, "I'm going to be the friendliest girl who ever hit that campus. I'm going to every school function and I'm going to accept every date, no matter how crummy the guy is. I'm going to circulate, I'm going to be seen! Maybe if I circulate enough and get seen enough, I'll start getting dates with guys I like."

Alice, as friendly in a nonsexy way as a puppy, began to circulate and began to be seen. She volunteered to make cakes and cookies for boys in a co-op house who were doing their own cooking. Since young men of college age will usually eat anything, especially when it's hot out of the oven, she always drew a crowd when odors of baking began to permeate the house. The boys adopted her as a kind of little sister, watched their language around her and saw to it that she had an escort whenever she needed one. By the end of the term her campaign had been so successful that her studies were suffering and she was compelled to cut down on her social activities. But by that time she had acquired a number of male as well as female friends, who liked her and felt at ease with her because she didn't attempt to play the siren.

[168]

When love develops out of a relationship of this kind, as it did with Alice, it is one of the tenderest and most beautiful experiences of a lifetime, whether or not it lasts. Hal won Alice's love and trust by always being thoughtful and considerate of her, and honorable and responsible in his dealings with others. She had won his love and admiration by being a good sport and delightful companion without throwing sex around. Her virginity aroused in him the respect and feeling of protectiveness which I think innocence will always evoke from responsible males. When he realized that their kisses were beginning to get a little warm, he would himself call a halt. So Alice was able to express her love for him without fear of getting into something neither wanted.

For sweet and beautiful as I have known and seen teen-age love to be, a couple must keep in mind that a person who fits our needs in the teens may not have the qualities we will want after we mature fully. If the first love does prove to be the one, that will become evident as the years go by. If not, my experience and observation have been that both are glad when they have kept the relationship one of affection, without the complications and heartaches that are likely to accompany the breakup of a sex relationship. Hal did prove to be the one in Alice's case, but she says, "In the teen years there's a lot to enjoy and see and understand and a lot of growing yet to be done. Sex is beautiful, but only when properly prepared for and after a lot of work at understanding yourself and the people around you. Don't rush it!"

Very, very best,
GLADYS SHULTZ

Books which describe the male and female reproductive organs and systems, together with other basic biological and psychological aspects of sex, are:

Hard Cover:

How to Understand Sex by Wayne J. Anderson, published by T. S. Denison & Co., Inc., 5100 West 82nd Street, Minneapolis, Minn. 55431; price $6.95. This company also publishes a full line of books covering sex problems, marriage and parenthood by the same author, who is Professor of Family Living at the University of Minnesota.

It's Time You Knew by Gladys Denny Shultz, with foreword by Somers H. Sturgis, M.D., Peter Bent Brigham Hospital, Boston, published by J. B. Lippincott Company, East Washington Square, Philadelphia, Pa. 19105, price $4.95.

Love and Sex in Plain Language by Eric W. Johnson, published by J. B. Lippincott Company, East Washington Square, Philadelphia, Pa. 19105; price $3.50.

Sex Before Twenty by Helen F. Southard, published by E. P. Dutton & Co., 201 Park Avenue, New York, N.Y. 10003; price $3.75. Add 40 cents for handling and postage, making a total of $4.15.

A very good paperback, costing $1.50, is *Teen-Age Counselor* by Bert Y. Glasser, M.D., published by Barron's Educational Series, Inc., 113 Crossways Park Drive, Woodbury, N.Y. 11797.

You may obtain free of charge a complete bibliography of books in the sex education field from Siecus (Sex Information and Education Council of the U.S.), 1855 Broadway, New York, N.Y. 10023.

Should Marriage Be for Keeps?

DEAR JANIE AND FRIENDS:

Back in the 1920's, when the divorce rate began to rise and Judge Ben Lindsey suggested that it would be a good idea for couples to live together for a period of time before going through a ceremony, in order to find out how congenial they are, he got into a peck of trouble.

Now that the divorce rate has approached the 50-per-cent mark, premarital sex has become part of the mores of at least part of the younger generation, and off-campus shacking up of unmarried students has been given official sanction by at least one women's college, once more the question has come up as to whether it is time to make some changes in our attitudes toward marriage. One leading authority, a woman, has speculated whether a middle-aged husband, for instance, should not be permitted to discard the wife of his youth for a newer model, presumably better fitted to the position he has attained. A good many middle-aged husbands have done this; the difference would be that under the new marriage code they would not need to suffer public disapproval.

That was why I offered for consideration two different plans for altering marriage, Plan 1 being that, before committing themselves to lifelong fidelity, a couple should announce their intention of "trying out" marriage for a period of time—two years, for instance—but refrain from having children. At the end of the period they would either go through the traditional ceremony or separate without the trouble and expense of divorce.

The replies and comments reveal wide divergences of opinion. Teen-age boys approved the idea of a trial marriage by a small majority, but the only comment made in favor of it was that the idea was good but the way it worked out would depend upon the individuals involved. One who disapproved said, "If two people are with each other enough they should be able to tell whether or or not they are in love. This living with each other is not right."

Men twenty and over rated the idea "not so good" by a narrow margin, those who approved giving such reasons as "a good way to get to know someone" and "a good idea, but it could also lead to widespread love-ins without the presence of love. Living together could become just another fad." One who vetoed the idea did so because he objected to solemnizing the union in any way. "Why go through a standard ritual—it's what we're trying to avoid. Living together is good. There should be no time limit, however." Another who questioned the time limit asked, "Why shouldn't they be free to come and go—to try several different arrangements? I agree with the abstention from having children until marriage, purely from the point of view that children would tend to make a couple stick together when they won't necessairly want to." Several thought it made more sense to "step down reactions to divorce proceedings. Divorce is not as tragic as it seems."

A considerable number find the idea "not so good" for exactly opposite reasons. "It goes against what God and the Bible says." "It would be no different from having no marriage at all. This is really free sex. You just change partners every two years." And "I'd kind of like a virgin—if I could get one—and with the pill a girl could live with a different guy every year."

Among teen-age girls, who split even between its being a good idea and not so good, those finding it a good idea made such comments as "Institutionalizing love is ridiculous." "The idea is good for stopping unhappy marriages and divorces, but I believe intercourse is *only* for marriage."

The teen-age girls who were against the idea made many more comments than those who thought it worthy of consideration. "If you're not sure a guy is for you, it's stupid and sinning to live with him," came from a sixteen-year-old high school senior. And from another girl, "Not too many guys would be attracted to a girl who had lived with someone for two years."

A number of this group mentioned the possibility of one of the couple being hurt very badly. "Some find it easy to run from one person to another; others become more emotionally involved and cannot react in the same way as the 'more free' partner."

A number called attention to the difficulty of carrying out the stipulation that there should be no children, a nineteen-year-old adding that, with divorce so widely accepted and so easy, there would be little difference from the present married state.

There were many expressions along the line of "An awful idea! Either you love the man and want to marry him or you don't." "Immature kids with little responsibility will never settle down." "The idea would certainly be misused. Too many people would jump at the idea of having a *legal* excuse for shacking up." "Marriage is to grow in love for each other while you grow older." "Human beings need to have a commitment to one another to be happy." "The whole purpose of living together is to be married and have children. It's not a 'do your own thing' situation as merely living together would seem to suggest." A seventeen-year-old high school senior thinks that the relationship "would just dwindle on, causing emotional and mental anxiety between the two people."

Girls twenty and over turned down the proposition by a ratio of 12 to 1, one of the miniscule minority objecting to any formalizing of the relationship. "I believe in some premarital sex, if couples want it, to see if they are compatible, but it should be a private agreement."

Quite a number of those opposed felt, like many of the teen-age girls, that someone was likely to get hurt and it was most likely to be the girl. "I know some who are doing this now and others who have done it and they wind up confused and hurt in the end. Or at least the girl did." Many of the older girls brought up the possibility of pregnancy as settling the matter.

Rather oddly, no one mentioned abortion in this connection, as had been done by the majority in the answers to my questions about the responsibility of the male in premarital or casual sex, though a great many brought up the matter of responsibility. "Emotions can't be played with so much. Marriage has responsibilities which often make it work rather than fall apart." "To make a success of marriage takes *total* devotion, and a halfway try just won't make it work." "The couple wouldn't try as hard and give as much to keep love going and growing." "A great portion of marriage is the acceptance of responsibility which this method denies." Several say they still hold to the traditional view of "finding the 'right one,' marrying and living happily. I don't think one has to live with someone first in order to know him well."

One from this group says, "People will fail to develop family relationships, due to the knowledge that they don't have to make it last, and will fail to take the trouble to try for success. Often marriage has problems but these problems are solved because of the relationship. In trial marriage, people will not make an attempt to communicate and solve the problems but rather say, 'Well, I guess it won't work' and go on to the next attempt. Although I don't agree with divorce methods, they are a restraining force to help people make an attempt to solve their problems before they give up."

There was much more unanimity in the replies to the second plan for altering marriage which I have seen proposed, that the sacramental feature should be dropped altogether in favor of a legal contract, as in a business connection for five or ten years, to be terminated at expiration without court proceedings, if one or both wanted out, or renewed for another limited period.

Boys under twenty split very nearly evenly between approval and disapproval, but those twenty and over turned it down by a ratio of 2 to 1, girls under twenty by a ratio of 11 to 1 and girls twenty and over by 12 to 1—though several of the last-named group objected on the basis that marriage should be done away with entirely. "It should be a personal thing, un-regimented and unlicensed."

The great majority, however, taken as a whole, expressed a desire to keep marriage as it is, a sacrament and an expression of undying love. Only one out of all who replied, a seventeen-year-old high school girl, pointed out that a marriage ceremony *is* a legal contract, in that it must be licensed and performed by an official of the church or state in the presence of witnesses, and people can't free themselves of the obligation they have assumed without going into court and convincing a judge or jury that one of the couple has behaved badly enough to warrant breaking the contract.

Many protested against the "dehumanizing effect" of removing the sacramental aspect and felt that it would take the beauty and sacredness out of the marriage relationship. "I believe a marriage needs God." "There are too many family break-ups now due to lack of strong ties. This would just increase the potential for marriages of convenience." "God will be a big part of my marriage. Many people go wrong when they leave this out." "They won't try so hard to make marriage work, and what happens to the children? If they always use the pill, what happens to the human race?"

That the majority want the solemn marriage vows to mean just what they say was further indicated by replies to the question I asked in connection with the statement about making love in the home playroom, which was rejected so emphatically by both younger and older respondents, that if the answer was yes to the playroom proposition, should it be made legitimate also for parents to make love with others than their lawful mates under the family roof? Since the great majority had said in no uncertain terms that they didn't want to make love in the home playroom or in the college dormitory either, not many replied to this. Of those who did, teen-age boys rejected the proposition by more than 2 to 1, males twenty and over by just under 2 to 1, teen-age girls unanimously and girls twenty and over by 3 to 1. The comments made stressed the sacredness of marriage, that it is for one male and one female only, and that if a man and woman can't be true to each other, they shouldn't marry. "Marriage is a bond between two people. If or when love dies to the extent of 'making love' with another, the marriage should be discontinued. A number spoke of the psychological harm done to youngsters who discover that the father or mother has an outside interest, others felt that "marriage is a commitment to a lasting and growing relationship with another person" and one teen-age girl wrote simply, "They're *married!*"

However, the harvest of suggestions I received for ways to prevent the present trend toward divorce was scanty. One girl believes it is through much greater sex freedom, "sexual relationships before marriage, or living together for a certain period of time prior to marriage as a prelude toward making the relationship permanent." Other suggestions were to "emphasize family life and the ability to accept people for what they are and believe," "to be really sure that marriage is really what you want and that you are really in love," "not to think of *self* so much but to help others become one large family."

I certainly can't find fault with the majority opinion that marriage, when entered into, should be based on real and lasting love and will be "until death do us part." I think of couples I know, some of whom have been married fifty years or more, growing old together, the wife who shared the early struggles and hardships now sharing the rewards, attuned to each other's little ways and needs and desires, enjoying their children and grandchildren together. Some of the marriages have weathered heavy storms, but I think in all these cases the couples are glad now that they stuck it out.

If one of a couple proves to be a monster or with habits or character defects which make him or her a harmful influence for the children, then divorce is indicated. But it always seems tragic to me when two good people, who loved each other when they married, both of whom love their children and are loved by their children, let all this go down the drain. Quite often it is because of immaturity. In such cases divorced persons who have learned to conquer childish traits that caused their unhappiness in the first marriage, and to be more tolerant of a mate's trifling idiosyncrasies, have made a success of second marriages. But how much better if they had made the effort the first time, particularly when children are involved.

I also agree with the majority opinion that a marriage is more likely to succeed if a couple refrains from outside entanglements. That was one phase of the new morality, as explained by the young man quoted in Letter IX, that bothered me—his statement that one can have a sex relationship with more than one person at a time, as long as one loves and respects all the sex partners. This is an idea that goes way back in history. Solomon, for instance, could always find room in his heart for one more. The Bible doesn't tell us, though, what the feelings of Wife No. 999 were when he started dedicating his love lyrics to Wife No. 1,000, or what the emotions of the thousand wives were when the Queen of Sheba appeared on the scene.

I knew a couple in the 1920's who boasted that both had affairs with full knowledge of the other and compared notes after their assignations. By 1930 they were divorced and had left town. I knew another couple who, after prosperity hit— there I go again!—adopted much the same program and were still together at last reports. But when they were young and hard up and crazy about each other, neither would have thought of such a thing.

Certainly the greater sex freedom suggested by several young cooperators is not the answer. A lawyer who specializes in divorce was quoted in early 1970 as saying that, among the younger couples, "there are none of the old hang-ups about sex that plagued marriages even ten years ago. These girls know all about orgasms from the age of fourteen." Nevertheless he gave sexual incompatibility as one of the principal reasons for divorce, along with in-laws and finances—"they're always short of money." He was quoted as saying, "only half jokingly," that all that women want is sex. It must be remembered that the women he was talking about were all wanting out of their marriages. According to my personal observations and what I read and hear, the more sex there has been in a young girl's life, the poorer her chances for a happy, lasting marriage, as a general rule.

I want to repeat here my appreciation of the honesty a number of you have shown in expressing thoughts contrary to the old moral concepts. It is not with any idea of putting down these people that I challenge some of their statements; it is simply that there would be no point in my going into this unless I were equally honest.

[178]

Let me also repeat that I do not hold the young responsible for what appear to me to be misconceptions. The old morality has put up a pretty feeble defense, if any, and your generation is entitled to more valid reasons for rejecting the *Playboy* philosophy than it has been given in most instances.

I would say that next to the illusion that personal happiness depends on knowledgeability and expertise in sex, the most damaging delusion fed the young is that marriage will solve all one's problems. Many a girl who married to get away from home returns home before long to get away from her marriage. Many a girl who married to avoid having to support herself finds herself drudging away in a poorly paid and uninteresting job because she hasn't prepared herself for better ones. As for the young man in the case, if a girl has any idea that he is going to change ways she doesn't like after they are married, she had better forget it.

One of the twenty-and-older girls noted in another connection the desirability of giving more attention to the selection of a mate, and I heartily agree with this, if marriages are to last and couples are to be unfailingly faithful to each other. A young man in the twenty-and-over group has seconded a suggestion that lovers should replace wishful thinking by a thorough study of the factors that make for success or failure in marriage, before they commit themselves. He says, "I think this is the most important thing of all. Sex education is very important, but mate selection is a phase of the scene that is not emphasized sufficiently, even though there is a lot of information."

As this young man says, the personality, character and background factors which make for success or failure of a marriage have been pinpointed by many researches, such as those of Lewis M. Terman, Burgess and Wallin, and Harold T. Christensen, to name just a few. Burgess and Wallin even give a scale for predicting the success or failure of a contemplated marriage in their book *Engagement and Marriage*, based on a study of 1,000 engaged couples and 666 married ones.* The younger an engaged couple are, the better advised they would be to inform themselves about material of this kind before marrying and, I would add, before entering into premarital sex—now that so many brides today are pregnant, indicating the extent to which sex is forcing marriages that perhaps would not have taken place otherwise, at least at that time.

The girl contemplating premarital sex might also ask herself, "Do I want my lover to get his first impression of me as a wife when I'm dragging around, feeling awful and looking awful, and maybe feeling guilty besides because he had to marry me?" For though pregnancy is a normal condition, a great many women experience considerable discomfort in the first three months, when the female body is adjusting itself to the tremendous task of creating a new life. It doesn't make for a very hilarious honeymoon.

After the first three months, if the pregnancy follows a normal course, the woman who is happy in her motherhood develops a glow and radiance, and her face gets lovelier with the knowledge that the baby to which she is looking forward eagerly is desired as ardently by her husband, whose concern for her makes the afflictions easier to bear.

This is the way I have seen it happen, over and over, when a couple waited for marriage, and presumably for sex as well, until they were in a position to become parents, or waited after marriage to start a family until they were in a position for a baby to be a boon instead of a burden.

But suppose the young husband has had to sacrifice plans and ambitions, assume a responsibility he is not yet equipped to carry handily, and the girl he loved has turned into a wan, dispirited ghost of herself, unable to get up in the morning

* *Editor's Note:* A popular version of this work, entitled *Courtship, Engagement and Marriage*, was written by Gladys Denny Shultz.

for fear of upchucking, having to sleep so much and feeling so rotten that household tasks go by the board?

Some friends of mine had an apartment next to a couple who were expecting one of those "premature" babies now so popular, that are miraculously born with every sign of having been carried to full term. The husband and wife quarreled all the time when he was at home. After the baby was born it cried nearly all the time, whether the father was home or not, but cried hardest when the parents were quarreling. I'll let you make your own estimate of the prospects for the happiness of both the marriage *and* the offspring in that particular case.

Very best again,
GLADYS SHULTZ

LETTER 15.

Marijuana, LSD and Other Drugs

DEAR JANIE AND FRIENDS:

When it comes to the new drug cult, I have to confess that I must operate entirely upon what I read and hear. I don't even belong to the adult cult of tranquilizers, cathartics, pills to aid digestion, pills to put one to sleep at night and pills to get one going in the morning, the only experience I ever had along this line having occurred in the mid-1940's. I was starting a head cold, had a very busy schedule, and asked a druggist for something to abort the cold. He sold me an inhaler, a medicated tube to stick up one's nostrils, and I inhaled it sedulously.

That night I really and truly didn't "sleep a wink" but didn't care, so many earth-shaking ideas were thronging through my mind, and I got up the next morning as alert and brisk as though I had had the regulation eight hours. Throughout breakfast I held forth with what I considered to be great brilliance and talked my way steadily through the rest of the day. It wasn't until the bottom fell out that evening that I read the fine print on the inhaler and found it contained Benzedrine, one of the amphetamines. So *that* was the reason people had been giving me peculiar looks all day long!

"You were on speed!" one of my on-the-spot consultants exclaimed. "It makes you talk a blue streak. Speed is one of the bad ones!" One experience was enough for me.

When a number of my young cooperators cited drugs as among the most critical questions before young girls today, I thought I ought to smoke a marijuana cigarette or two to find out for myself what their effect is. Then I was told that to obtain marijuana legally, for research purposes, one must apply to a Federal bureau in Washington, D.C., and go through all manner of red tape, a process requiring months; and if I were to obtain it any other way, not only would I be liable to a prison term but so would the person from whom I had obtained the cigarettes, so I gave that up.

However, I have been reading a great deal and listening to people who have dealt with young drug users, and to young users themselves who have appeared on radio panels. Also I am well acquainted with the adult cigarette-liquor pattern with which many of the young compare the pot-LSD cult. As a doctor who has treated many young drug users says, even young people who don't use drugs will be faced with the temptation and will need good, legitimate reasons for refraining, so I'll do the best I can.

First I'll report the reactions of my young helpers to a statement one sees frequently, that "the great majority of college students and many high schoolers have experimented with a psychedelic or hallucinogenic drug." Teen-age boys split exactly even between "true" and "untrue," one saying it was true at the Eastern men's college he attends; males twenty and over gave "true" a majority by slightly under 3 to 2; teen-age girls said "true" by a little under 3 to 2 and girls twenty and over, "true" by a little over 3 to 2, one saying it is true at least in the East and West. Slightly under one fifth of all those replying indicated that they had tried pot or some other drug in the categories mentioned, either by saying they had or by refraining from checking six suggested reasons I had offered for not having tried any. One of the twenty-and-over boys said he had tried marijuana but not the others, his chief reason being that he feared they might harm him. A teen-age girl said she knows people who have tried both marijuana and the harder drugs, "but they are not in the majority."

We perhaps get a truer picture of what the "silent majority" of the young think on the subject from the reasons for refraining checked by the slightly over 80 per cent who had abstained. As a group, males twenty and over who had never indulged had been least deterred by moral consideration, fear of being caught, parental disapproval and lack of opportunity (access to drugs, that is) and most influenced by fear that a drug would harm them and by not wanting to.

Girls twenty and over also were least deterred by moral considerations, fear of being caught and lack of opportunity; they were most deterred by not wanting to and fear it might harm them, but more of them were influenced than were the older males by moral considerations and parental disapproval.

The growing availability of marijuana for younger Americans is indicated by the fact that teen-age boys were least deterred by fear of getting caught and lack of opportunity—in fact only two checked this reason—and most deterred by fear of being harmed, not wanting to, moral considerations and parental disapproval.

Teen-age girls, unlike the other groups, split fairly evenly between being deterred and not deterred by moral considerations, fear it might harm them, lack of opportunity, not wanting to and parental disapproval. The only marked divergence from fairly equal distribution between deterrence and nondeterrence was that only one half as many checked fear of being caught for deterrence as for nondeterrence.

A girl in the twenty-and-older group said, "The statement posed depends on the social class you are considering. It is *basically* true in the upper-middle-class and upper-income suburbs but not necessarily in the intercity population on a college campus. Drug usage is prevalent, but by no means everyone has taken drugs or smoked pot. Really I find it is only a small minority."

One of the twenty-and-older males added an additional deterring factor: "I consider drugs psychologically harmful to certain types of personalities." Another of this group says, "I have never tried because I have no desire to ruin my future. I have no reason to escape from reality, because I have a happy home and great love between my parents and between my sisters and myself."

A number of the feminine abstainers saw no point in trying drugs. "It might be interesting, but so what? Other things are more interesting and gratifying." Several stressed the theme of "I was busy with books and people, and I was afraid I would regret it." "I don't feel that I need it. I can become very 'high' by experiencing meaningful and warm relations with people. I can face reality most of the time and don't feel I need an escape."

The abstainers have made so many important points that I am tempted to stop right here. However, there are some vexing questions, especially about marijuana, and such a large proportion of teen-agers and younger children are being exposed that we should look at these.

I don't think there is any question that there is a difference between the occasional use of marijuana and experimentation with LSD, heroin or the various stimulants, depressants, psychedelics and hallucinogenics that have been added to our pharmacopeia in recent years, which can have serious consequences. I can very well believe the comment of a teen-age girl that "many try marijuana just to see what it's like, so they can condone or condemn it fairly, with no intention of continuing or of using other drugs. They try this particular one because it is particularly mild and harmless."

I doubt there were many boys of my generation who hadn't tried cigarettes out of curiosity, and I know for a fact that a number of girls of my generation started smoking in the 1920's for the very reason that older people considered it immoral for women to smoke and we didn't think morals had anything to do with it.

So I asked a psychiatrist at a state university if smoking marijuana were not the "thing" of many of this young generation, just as smoking cigarettes was the "thing" for a number of my generation. He said no, it wasn't; that the young smoke marijuana for the feeling of euphoria or the illusion of heightened perception they get from it. Only those who have tried marijuana can say which concept is the correct one.

The really burning questions are hotly disputed. One trouble is that there has been no research into the effects of marijuana comparable to that which revealed, to the satisfaction of most medical authorities, that regular cigarettes can kill you. A former head of the Department of Health, Education and Welfare was even quoted as saying that he saw no harm in marijuana. But in 1968, the Committee on Problems of Drug Dependence of the National Research Council and the Committee on Alcoholism and Drug Dependence of the American Medical Association issued a joint report on marijuana, based on findings of doctors who had had considerable experience in treating users of the drugs which have come fashionable of late. It held that cannabis, the scientific name for marijuana, "is a dangerous drug and is a public health concern. Practically all societies in which it is extensively used have found it necessary to impose legal and social sanctions on users and distributors. Although it is not addictive, it is a powerful psychoactive agent [affecting one's mental state] and where chronic heavy use occurs it often has a marked effect in reducing the social productivity of the user." An earlier study defined chronic heavy use as smoking six to eight marijuana cigarettes a day.

A study by McGlothlin and West, published in the *Ameri-*

can Journal of Psychiatry for September, 1968, found that regular use of marijuana "contributes to apathy, loss of effectiveness, and inability to carry out long-range plans. Such users had a low capacity to endure frustration, poor concentration, impaired verbal facility, and a strong tendency to regressive, childlike, magical thinking. . . . They appeared to be totally involved with the present at the expense of future goals."

On the other hand, a number of doctors point out that marijuana used to be widely used in medicine, as a mild muscle relaxant and anticonvulsant, and was contained in many non-prescription, over-the-counter medications until 1937, when the law was passed making it illegal. I read that at that time the American Medical Association suggested that it might be worthwhile to keep cannabis among the medications "for such purposes as it now has."

However, there seems to be general agreement on the symptoms exhibited by marijuana smokers. Paul N. Seward, M.D., is a young Harvard Medical School graduate who took his period of elective training for pediatrics in the Haight-Ashbury Clinic in San Francisco, where a survey of 500 persons selected from clinical patients, habitués of cafés in the area and people on the street revealed that 94.5 per cent were users of marijuana and 87.8 percent of LSD; 44.5 per cent were taking methedrine, an amphetamine, by mouth and 26.5 per cent by injection, with 24.8 per cent on heroin. He contributed an extremely informative article to the October, 1969, issue of the *Harvard Medical Alumni Bulletin*, in which he gave the chemical make-up of the drugs named and the effects they produce on the minds and bodies of users.

Dr. Seward described the marijuana symptoms as a mild tachycardia, or speeding up of heart action, also true of ordinary cigarettes; runny nose; reddened eyes; mouth dryness; rather marked hunger, especially for sweets; and ataxia, which is failure in muscular coordination, the thing that makes a drunk person reel around.

"Psychologically it induces lethargy and mild euphoria; there may be disturbances in perception of time and space, increased receptivity if not sensitivity to tactile sensations and a subjective increase in imagination and perception," the last meaning that the user thinks his powers of imagination and perception have increased, as I thought while influenced by Benzedrine, but that it isn't necessarily so. Dr. Seward says that these symptoms gradually fade after two or three hours, "leaving a mild feeling of calm and passivity for several hours more, though this last effect is probably due more to the attitude of the user than to the drug." Because of the changed mental state the drug brings about, Dr. Seward conceives that it might be possible for a user to harm himself while under its influence but that it is not very likely. Other observers say that no deaths have ever been reported from marijuana.

An experiment conducted at the Boston University School of Medicine confirmed the symptoms described by Dr. Seward, and it was additionally reported that while the marijuana smokers got high and experienced great changes in their perception of things around them, their behavior gave no indication that they were high and observers couldn't tell they were. However, other studies have reported a tendency for the smoker to get giggly and talkative and note that it affects individuals differently, some reacting much more strongly than others to the same amount. I read that marijuana is not addictive—but that's what we were told about ordinary cigarettes—that there has been no evidence of physical harm in users studied to date, but no one knows yet what effect habitual use over a long period of time may have on body organs.

I can't remember ever having heard of marijuana, though the plant grew wild on roadsides and in vacant lots in the area where I grew up, until the 1930's when I read that it was smoked by members of jazz bands in order to keep up the furious tempo throughout an evening. Then in 1941 Gene Krupa, the star drummer of the era, served a jail sentence for possessing it. In November, 1969, Mr. Krupa came out of seclusion to tell a group of teen-agers what marijuana had done for him. "I suppose like every other kid I thought it would better my playing, but that was an hallucination." He said he discovered this when he heard a record he had made while under the influence of marijuana. "I found it was pretty bad. You think you are playing good—you think you're beating up a storm, but you're not." The marijuana had distorted time, he said, as noted by Dr. Seward, "and time is the essence to a drummer."

The second burning question, and one that I find the young are very sensitive to, is whether or not smoking marijuana leads to experimenting with the stronger and admittedly harmful and addictive drugs. While heroin use is increasing alarmingly, it is as yet by no means in proportion to the increase in marijuana use. On the other hand, a good many people have confessed they had started with marijuana, gone on to LSD and then to heroin, and a study of twenty-one LSD users in a men's college showed that all had started with marijuana. We are told that many marijuana smokers are now turning to hashish, a much stronger form of cannabis, which gets its name from the Arabic word meaning "assassin." You have probably read of the Assassin cult which murdered many heads of state and other people in Persia and Syria in the twelfth and thirteenth centuries A.D., its professional executioners being turned into murderous automatons by hashish; and of the dervishes of the late nineteenth century, a sect which used hashish for the same purpose before going into battle. Not long ago some cured heroin addicts told a group of junior schoolers about the degradation of being a addict and of the danger of going on to stronger drugs from marijuana. "You think you won't, but that's what we thought," was the burden of their message.

And now to compare regular cigarettes and liquor with what I have gleaned about marijuana. The damage regular cigarettes do is physical. I have known people who smoked as many as three to four packs, or sixty to eighty cigarettes, a day, with no discernible change in their mental powers or personalities, though eventually their health was affected. The physical damage comes from heavy smoking, defined as ten or more cigarettes a day, over a long period of time. To date, the chief victims of lung cancer have been men, simply because fewer women became habitual smokers at as early an age as the average male smoker did.

From my own experience, and that of many others, I could not honestly say that it would hurt anyone to smoke a few cigarettes now and then, as long as one didn't smoke heavily or regularly enough to get hooked, but I would implore my young friends not to get hooked!

It is true that tobacco is not addictive in the way that heroin is and the withdrawal agonies are by no means as horrendous. But let us imagine now that you become a chronic smoker and you develop a hacking cough or shortness of breath or your blood pressure goes up and your doctor tells you you will have to quit smoking. You will find it isn't easy. And even when you have gone through all the pangs of quitting and, feeling you can take it or leave it, smoke just one cigarette, you can get hooked all over again. A friend of mine tells me he still feels an urge to smoke, though he hasn't smoked for eighteen years.

I have always considered regular cigarettes the mildest of the vices, but they don't do anybody any good, and it is wiser never to start. If one has started, my advice would be, don't carry cigarettes; and if one should begin to feel an urge to associate a smoke with more and more activities of the day, stop keeping them in the house.

Nor could I honestly say to my young friends what I was taught when I was young, that to take a drink of alcohol will lead straight to a drunkard's grave. In adult life I have known too many people for whom the cocktail or highball or two before the meal and wine during it are as much a part of civilized dining as the coffee afterwards, who never lose control and live to a ripe old age. I have also known people who died at comparatively young ages because they misused alcohol.

The danger of alcohol consists, on the one hand, of exceeding one's capacity, getting drunk and perhaps killing one or more persons in a driving accident, or committing some other type of serious offense such as rape or homicide, and this can happen on the only occasion that a person has drunk an intoxicant. It has been found that around one half of the violent rapes are triggered by alcohol. It gets in its deadly work, on the other hand, when people turn to it every time they feel unhappy or experience a little setback, instead of facing and dealing with the problem. This is the road to alcoholism, which can ruin a life and has ruined many lives. It damages one physically, aside from the accidents that occur from drunkenness, when alcoholics drink, instead of eating, as alcoholics have a tendency to do. This can produce cirrhosis of the liver, a frequently fatal disease.

Sometimes a host with a mistaken sense of hospitality will urge liquor upon a guest or even fill up a guest's glass after he or she has declined. Don't drink it! Responsible people respect the wishes of others not to drink anything spirituous, or to stop when they know they have had enough.

It would seem logical that the potential for harm of marijuana would be of the same variety. If one used it to get the feeling of euphoria or altered perceptions mentioned by many authorities, there might well be a temptation to go for bigger and better reactions provided by the stronger drugs; or if one used it to take the edge off difficulties, as has been mentioned by various investigators, one could easily become a chronic user, with the adverse effects described previously. This could be a particular temptation for adolescents, Dr. Seward points out, if they use it "to avoid the conflicts of young adulthood, and as a means of postponing their resolution until such behavior perhaps becomes habitual." But he says it is still a matter of debate whether this actually happens.

After weighing the evidence for and against, I would be tempted to conclude that if marijuana were not illegal, there could conceivably be no more harm in occasionally smoking marijuana in company with others, for sociability, then in occasionally smoking regular cigarettes, provided one didn't let it become a habit and didn't ever smoke enough to lose touch with reality or to affect coordination. But it *is* illegal, and that makes a great big difference.

In California alone, where anyone over eighteen can draw a prison term of from one to ten years for mere possession, more than 28,000 adults were arrested on this charge in a single year, while 94 per cent of the juvenile arrests the same year were for possessing marijuana or other drugs. There are some causes important enough to humanity to justify breaking a law and going to jail or prison, as the Reverend Martin Luther King did a number of times. But is marijuana such a cause?

It is true that, as in other cases where penalties are way out of line with the offense, many judges will give a young person a suspended sentence for marijuana possession. Nevertheless, as I have pointed out to men in prisons with whom my work has brought me in touch, when we break a law that we consider unjust or to avenge ourselves for some wrong we feel society has done to us, we put ourselves at the mercy of society, and a judge who takes a dim view of narcotics might invoke the full penalty.

I wonder how many of the young who smoke marijuana out of curiosity or rebellion against adult society realize the possible consequences of being convicted of possessing marijuana, whether or not the judge were to give a suspended sentence. The most complete list I have found is in a novel, *Dress Her in Indigo*, by John D. MacDonald. He points out that since possession is a felony under American law, an eighteen-year-old, picked up with just two marijuana cigarettes on him and convicted, can lose the right to vote, the right to own a gun, and the right to run for public office, and that is only the beginning. "He can never become a doctor, dentist, C.P.A., engineer, architect, realtor, osteopath, physical therapist, private detective, masseur or stockbroker. He can never get any job where he has to be bonded or licensed. He can't work for the city, county or federal governments. He can't get into West Point, Annapolis or the Air Force Academy. He can enlist in the military but will be denied his choice of services and probably will be assigned to a labor battalion." I can add that not only would the person be barred from the Air Force Academy, he—or she—could not enlist in the Air Force.

But to me, there are even more potent reasons. For one thing, I have found that there are many practical advantages in staying on the right side of the law. For instances, if one does become involved in a criminal situation in any way, even as an innocent victim, to have an unblemished record is a pearl beyond price. As long as we have clean hands, to use the legal phrase, we can protest against injustice with might and main, in public speeches, in letters to the newspapers, to our representatives in the state legislature and Congress and to the President himself. But if we have been convicted of a crime, people are likely to say, "Look who's talking."

Even more important, to buy illicit drugs is to ally ourselves with the monsters who reap millions out of the traffic and ruin and destroy promising young lives with no more compunction than if they were so many mosquitoes or flies. The bootleggers and rumrunners of prohibition days seem almost saintly in comparison. In the 1920's, there were gang wars, hijacking of liquor consignments and a good deal of bumping off of rival gangsters, with an occasional innocent bystander getting killed by a stray bullet. But the gangsters of that day didn't hang around grade and junior and senior high schools, passing out free samples in order to make drinkers and customers out of youngsters.

Today's drug traffickers stop at nothing. In New York City, it was discovered that a man had been injecting heroin hypodermically into ten-year-olds and one eight-year-old girl. But even more chilling than this was a report that some students at Columbia University were grossing from $1,200 to $3,000 a month dealing in marijuana, LSD, mescaline, hashish and amphetamines. A senior at Barnard, the women's college affiliated with Columbia, was arrested on a charge of having in her apartment a store of drugs which it was estimated would bring $100,000 on the market. An undergraduate was quoted as saying that while students didn't go in much for heroin or cocaine as a rule, she thought they were inclined to experiment with these terribly dangerous drugs when there was a shortage of marijuana or hashish. This would tend to confirm that use of one of the mind-distorting drugs can lead to experimentation with stronger ones.

The average drug pusher on the street is often an addict himself, getting money to support his own habit, and poorly educated. But college students can hardly be ignorant of the harmful potential of the drugs some are said to be selling. A year or two previous to the disclosure of the campus drug trafficking, a Columbia student, the scion of a very prominent family, had died of heroin, to which it was reported he had progressed through marijuana and LSD. Only a few months previously a Barnard girl had died from heroin—one overly strong dose can be fatal—and the daughter of a well-known entertainer had killed herself in New York City by jumping out of a high window while under the influence of LSD. One LSD death and a number of reactions serious enough to need medical treatment were reported from the greatly publicized Woodstock festival in the summer of 1969.

In case not all of the younger people know the effects of the drugs named, let's take a brief look at them. Under LSD, the user can lose all touch with reality, becoming temporarily insane, and not all who go on LSD trips regain their sanity. Dr. Seward says that the manifestations may take many forms but often for the user it is a terrible nightmare, and patients frequently complain that they are going to disintegrate, "that if they relax for an instant their mind will destroy itself in a wave of disorder."

I have already described my own experience with amphetamines, and I got off very easily compared with the things "speed" can do to you. According to Dr. Seward, a very small amount of methedrine, the amphetamine most used in the Haight-Ashbury section, can produce the form of insanity called paranoia, or delusions of persecution, aberrant or "crazy" behavior, and hallucinations. The oral form is bad enough, but a considerable proportion progress to "mainlining," injecting it into a vein with a hypodermic needle.

Dr. Seward says that the average amphetamine user is young, and comes to the clinic because of a mental disturbance or hepatitis, usually incurred through use of a contaminated hypodemic needle, or for abscesses, also incurred from needles. He draws a horrifying picture of a nineteen-year-old addict who had had his frontal, or forehead, bone and one eye removed as result of infection, was thirty pounds underweight, had

[195]

numerous abscesses on his arms and hands and still had no desire to be cured of the habit.

As for heroin and cocaine, their addictive, death-dealing, crime-inducing properties are so well known that I don't see how any intelligent, educated person could think of toying with them who had not acquired a craving for synthetic thrills or escape from reality through experiments with the less lethal varieties.

There is such vigorous protest against lumping marijuana with drugs like these that I think the law will surely be changed and the penalties either removed or greatly lessened for possessing or smoking it. But whether or not marijuana should be legalized is a tough one. The joint report of the drug committees of the National Research Council and American Medical Association cited previously recommended that the penalties for use be made more realistic but warned against legalization, on the ground that this "would probably create a serious abuse problem in the United States. Currently used hemp products are of low potency, but if controls were eliminated, more potent (and dangerous) preparations would probably dominate the legal market."

However, attempts to enforce the present laws apparently have accomplished little except to acquaint thousands of teen-agers as well as older people with police courts and jails and to make so much money for the illicit purveyors that college students are getting into the racket, regardless of the effect the drugs they sell can have on their student customers.

On this account I would be inclined to go along with a suggestion that marijuana be made legal for those eighteen and over, under the same restrictions that now govern the sale of cigarettes and alcoholic beverages. That is to say, dealers must be licensed and are subject to penalties if caught selling to persons under the legal age. This system has proved fairly effective with alcohol. I know that restaurants and liquor stores are very careful about selling liquor to persons under the legal age, lest they lose their license; and while the vending machines make cigarettes available to anyone who has the money, I have never heard of cigarette smoking among youngsters to the degree that the young are now going in for marijuana.

The question remains as to how correct the two drug committees were in prophesying that legalization would probably lead to domination of the market by more potent and dangerous preparations. I am not being moralistic when I say that, to me, the most ominous sign for the future of our society is the participation in the traffic by privileged members of the young generation and the spread of the sex-drug cult into younger and younger groups, with marijuana and LSD apparently linked together like love and marriage in the song, and with sex following after, at least in some cases. At the famous Woodstock festival, we are told, part of the spirit of brotherly love exhibited was generosity in sharing marijuana and LSD, and sex as well. "Of course there was sex," a male participant told a reporter. "Only we waited until dark, out of consideration for the people who lived around there."

Researchers, attempting to determine whether it is true that LSD causes genetic mutation, followed 119 pregnant women —or I should say girls, for the average age was nineteen— through 127 pregnancies, starting as close to the time of conception as possible. The girls had been recruited from hippie colonies in the area but were from middle or upper class backgrounds and rather highly educated. More than half had tried drugs before they were eighteen, and all had taken LSD before or during their pregnancies.

It developed that they were very poor obstetrical risks. The 119 had 127 pregnancies while being studied but of these 43 percent ended in spontaneous abortion—expelling of an embryo without anything having been done to bring it about—as against a 20 to 25 per cent average in the general population; and in the 65 babies carried to full term the incidence of defects was eighteen times higher than in the general population.

However, the investigation didn't feel that the research had established the case against LSD because the girls had so many other things wrong with them which might have affected their unborn babies, including poor nutrition, use of other drugs in addition to LSD, and a history of illnesses such as hepatitis, frequently caused (as said before) because drug users will pass a hypodermic needle around a group, and venereal disease, associated with promiscuous sex. This was true of all the girls.

Drug users can be a menace to nonusers. In October of 1969, a nineteen-year-old University of Maryland student was acquitted of a charge of breaking and entering and attempted rape when it was shown that he had committed his crimes while temporarily insane from LSD which someone had, unknown to him, slipped into the soft drink he was consuming. In another instance reported in the papers the guests at a large party began acting so "crazy" that all were taken to a hospital. It was suspected that some joker had put LSD in the punch bowl, though according to Dr. Seward the symptoms of LSD poisoning can be so varied that diagnosis is difficult unless the victims are sufficiently oriented to be able to say they had taken LSD, and these people wouldn't have known they were taking it.

Not long ago I was talking to a woman who is engaged in mental health work and remarked that this is a very difficult time for the young to grow up in. She exclaimed, "How right you are! My son is a senior in college and I'm praying that he'll be able to graduate without something terrible happening. He's already had more narrow escapes than you would believe. Just a few weeks ago, he was at a party where the girl friend of one of his fraternity brothers appeared to have had too much to drink and he felt it was his duty to get her home safely. As they were driving to her dormitory, she reached into her purse, said 'Here's something for you,' and handed him a tablet. He realized then that she was high on a drug and that was what she had put in his hand.

"Just then a police car came along, and he said his heart sank into his boots. The police had been stopping cars containing young people and searching them for drugs. He knew he wouldn't have a ghost of a chance to get them to believe he was innocent. Fortunately the police car went on by, and Chuck went into the next filling station and flushed the tablet down the toilet. But one wonders how long his luck can hold."

My young cooperators have suggested a number of excellent ways to avoid the dangers inherent in drugs—enjoyment to the full of families and friends, books, music, and any of the many forms of physical activity that blow away mental problems, increase bodily welfare and vigor and have no unpleasant aftereffects. I can forget troubles in my work and, when my brain gets too tired for that, lose myself in reading suspense or detective stories or pulling up weeds or other outdoor activity. I don't think we need to be ashamed of escape hatches which do no harm to us or to anybody else.

I can also say from experience that every time we face a problem squarely and wrestle it to the ground we gain some measure of strength and skill for facing the next one, and that the great majority of difficulties which had seemed insuperable at the time will be forgotten six months hence. To escape into either drugs or liquor could create a very real continuing problem from which it would be very difficult to extricate oneself.

Whether or not marijuana is made legal, I would be wary myself of anything that clouds the mind, alters reality and affects one's behavior—and that goes for an excess of alcohol—unless it is prescribed by a doctor for a definite physical ailment. And I would also be wary of any person who offered me such a substance, for it indicates a serious lack of responsibility.

I heard a teen-age girl, a drug addict, say on a radio panel

[199]

where the drug problem was discussed, "I lost my teen years, I really feel I lost my teen age. And now that I have a baby, I know I can never get it back again."

If an associate or fellow guest at a party or a seemingly friendly adult were to offer you pot or a tablet of unknown nature "just so you can see what it's like," I think a proper reply would be, "Thank you, but no. I don't want to lose my teen years."

I'll devote my next letter to some unfinished business and questions and suggestions that have come in.

Very very best,
GLADYS SHULTZ

LETTER 16.

Preparing for an Uncertain Future

Dear Janie and Friends:

"But what's the use of doing anything?" a young man in one of the groups I have been conferring with suddenly exclaimed. "There isn't going to be any future. Within thirty years we're all going to be dead from air pollution or lack of pure water. Unless, that is, we're all killed off first by nuclear bombs or radiation sickness."

I agreed that no previous generation has ever faced a prospect like this one. But I pointed out that I can remember several periods since I grew up when it looked as though the end was approaching. There were bad times for agriculture in the 1920's, when farmers were growing desperate, the rate of armed robberies soared and there were race riots in Chicago. This period was followed by the Great Depression, which affected nearly everyone; and as we were beginning to pull out of that, Providence sent along several drought years. Dust from Oklahoma fields made drifts on porches in Des Moines, Iowa, and for a while it looked as though the whole Midwest, to which a considerable portion of the globe looks for food, would dry up and blow away.

In the early 1940's there was the black, black period when Britain, standing alone against the Axis, was threatened with invasion and the Axis occupied all the European mainland except Sweden, Switzerland and Portugal, which Hitler left alone because it served his purposes to do so, and Spain, whose government was sympathetic to the Axis; all the islands of the Mediterranean except Malta; Northern Africa nearly to Cairo and Iran in the Near East; all the islands of the Pacific except the Hawaiian group and tiny Wake; all of Eastern Asia except the interior of China; and were reaching toward Australia and India. We Americans were helpless because our people had been so sick of fighting after World War I that Congress had passed an act forbidding our government to do anything to help beleaguered friends, or do anything worse to aggressors than shake an admonitory finger at them, until we were attacked ourselves. And then a few years after this came the horrifying discovery that, unknown to any but those engaged on the project, a weapon had been developed which could wipe out all life on earth.

Yet so far none of the threatened calamities has come true. Anarchy didn't take over during the depression, the rains came, the Allies won World War II and, since Hiroshima and Nagasaki, no nuclear weapon has been used against an enemy.

Someone may say, "But it isn't just the United States that's in trouble. Students are rebelling in other Western and some Eastern countries; governments are being overthrown right and left. More countries are setting up nuclear reactors. Surely it was never like this before."

I think there is hope and comfort in the fact that this isn't the first time Western civilization has been thrown into general disarray. There was a period in Europe very similar to our present one, in the sixteenth and seventeenth centuries, when the old guidelines had been swept away and "a whole generation began to grow excited and argumentative and angry," as one writer expressed it (Harold Loukes, in the introduction to his book, *The Discovery of Quakerism*).

Previous to that time, the kings and nobles had done the thinking and decision making in temporal affairs for common mortals; the popes and clergy had had undisputed rule over religion and education. With the breaking down of the feudal system people began to think and make decisions for themselves, and when Martin Luther claimed the right for laymen to read and interpret the Bible, the challenges to authority became as widesweeping as the challenges to authority today. Yet both Western society and the Christian faith survived, though considerable alterations were made in the political, educational and religious systems.

Most encouraging, however, is that, except for nuclear warfare, about which we can only continue to hope and work for international controls, there is no problem confronting our society today which can't be solved by the application of human intelligence.

One of the girls in the group doubted that there is time left to do this. She said that her individual solution is to keep close to her idea of what's right and contribute what she can for others. "I'm in love with a wonderful guy, I have faith in people as individuals and will do whatever I can for them. I'm not going to deny life and love but will get all I can out of whatever life is going to be left to us."

By all means let's get all the happiness we can out of life, and most of us have many things to be happy about. But don't throw in the sponge! The fault is not with our system but with technological, scientific, industrial and social forces which have been allowed to run wild like cancer cells in an otherwise healthy body. Ralph Nader has shown what a single courageous, dedicated person can accomplish against the biggest and most strongly entrenched interests. The first question is, How can the oncoming generation best prepare itself to take an effective part in this battle?

One of the twenty-and-over young men challenged my suggestion that girls should wait for college until they have a clear conception of their ultimate goals. He said, "I don't yet have a clear conception of my ultimate goals even though I graduate from college this year. Also, for many people college is a way to acquire an understanding of one's goals, and delay decision making until they are more mature." And one of the girls asked me, "Have you thought about discussing education as a preparation for life, as opposed to training in a particular field; and how both education and training may be required for our future problems and tasks?"

Very good points indeed, and I would certainly not withold college from anyone who genuinely wants to broaden perspectives, get an idea of the different fields of human endeavor and the invaluable insights provided by history and literature and languages. I can think of no better preparation than a liberal arts course in college and then specialization. A college senior who plans to become a civil engineer agreed. "In any specialty there are times when other areas are necessary. For instance, the civil engineer should know sociology and political science. In future there will be a great need for civil engineers who are thinking in terms of people." I'd like to add that in a society at present so dominated by technology and science it would be well for sociologists, psychiatrists and the like to know enough about these fields to be aware of what the technological and scientific wizards are up to.

To cope with the kind of "progress" which has taken such toll of human concern, one of my young advisors suggested that an authority should be set up similar to the ones which now regulate specific sectors of our economy, but whose task would be to oversee the whole society, coordinate its many factors and keep them in balance, by passing upon new ideas and inventions before they are allowed to be put into use, as our Food and Drug Administration now has power to hold up use of new drugs until the manufacturers have proved that they are safe and needed. Thus such an authority might put a hold order on "advances" which would speed up our already too hectic life still further, take jobs and businesses away from many more millions in the interests of "economy"—that is to say, bigger dividends and earnings for a few—and medical discoveries like the new fertility drug which lately has caused four, five and six babies to be born from one pregnancy, surely the last thing our society needs at this point.

In recent years I have thought many times of D. H. Lawrence's statement that, when we solve a problem of the people, thirty more rise up to take its place. That has happened over and over since our government began to try to solve the problems of the people in the early 1930's, because well-meant programs were not always thoroughly thought through or were not abandoned after they had served their purpose because those who had been benefitting raised such a fuss.

We have already demonstrated that Americans can accomplish anything mechanical they take it into their heads to do, whether it is in space exploration or gadgetry. I agree heartily with those who say that the time has come to show what Americans can do toward providing a better world for the present generation to raise its children in.

I have been impressed by a theme running through the criticisms my young cooperators have made of parents, education and society: Their expressions of desire to be free, to get out from under restrictions and routines, to have a chance to learn what they are and what they want from life. In fact, finding an identity was named by quite a number as a principal question before teen-age girls today. Several of my young and adult cooperators have pointed out that our present society makes no use of youth, and I think that is a big reason for the dissatisfactions felt by so many young people and for the generation gap where it exists.

The bulk of your parents' generation, growing up during the depression, got a full taste of the realities of life. Moreover, the proliferation of gadgetry and automation didn't really get under way until after World War II. I first heard of identity crises in the late 1950's, when the children of the new prosperity began to hit the colleges.

The hard fact is that we can't be truly free and independent as long as we are dependent on anyone else for anything, and many of my young respondents acknowledged this in answering my question, "Do you think that an offspring's being dependent on parents financially, or living under the parental roof, entitles parents to expect compliance with certain rules of behavior, as hours to get in at night, etc.?" The answer was yes by a very considerable majority, with the notable exception of a young man in the twenty-and-over group who advised his peers to "Fight to the last! I did—and won!" I myself would agree with the minority who said that regulation should depend upon the age and maturity of the offspring and their need for guidance. But I suspect that the teen-age girl who replied that financial dependence shouldn't be a factor, but often is, hit the nail on the head for many others.

The desire for independence and freedom to find one's true self came through again in answers to my question, "Would you prefer to rear your children in an environment which emphasizes marriage and the good of the family above individual freedom and desires?" Quite a few interpreted the question, which I acknowledge was badly stated, as a matter of surrendering individuality by parents and children. What I had in mind was the kind of *outside* environment, the kind of community or neighborhood in which you would prefer to raise your children; whether one in which the majority of parents give first place to the mental, physical and emotional needs of the family or one where the ruling motif is the personal ambition of the parents to rise in business or social status, leading to the neglect of vital needs of their youngsters and to emptiness in their own lives which are being portrayed in modern novels about affluent city and suburban living.

Nevertheless, a considerable majority checked yes, and I am glad, for hard fact No. 2 is that the more ambitious we are to achieve material success, and the greater our appetite for prestige and luxuries, the less free we are bound to be. But no one can compel us to sacrifice ideals for the sake of a bigger pay check or to do anything contrary to our consciences, provided we are willing to accept the financial penalty for refusal to conform.

I have known people who got out of the rat race, as far as it is possible for moderns, by keeping their wants modest and developing their abilities to do for themselves. I am thinking in particular of three families who went together to buy a tract of land in California, moved out there in trailers and lived in the trailers while each family built its own house and a common building for the children to play in and the parents to entertain in, wives and children working alongside the husbands. Then the parents sold articles and books on how to build your own house.

These couples had not plunged into their venture blindly. All were writers who had sold, the husbands all had done carpentry as a hobby and one had already built a house. Also they had "slaved" in offices until they had accumulated the money to put their plan into operation. Still, it took courage to leave good jobs but none ever regretted it.

Paul Goodman has said that there should be a resettlement program in this country, and that would be my solution for our mounting welfare problem. To me it makes more sense to return displaced farm families to the land, where they can raise a considerable part of their food, keep chickens and a few pigs, maybe a cow and even a horse, our society supplying through taxes whatever is needed beyond this for a decent living standard, than to continue to pour out billions for the entire support of these families in slums and ghettos where the youngsters are exposed to drugs and every other form of vice.

Nor do I see how the vigor which once characterized Americans can be regained unless a considerable number of the more privileged also are willing to make whatever sacrifice of personal ambition is required to give their children open spaces, acquaintance with growing things and animals, and tasks at which the youngsters can work alongside the father and mother.

I am hoping very hard that a plan proposed by the late Frank Lloyd Wright and now being pushed by others will be put into effect—to dot the great empty spaces of our country with small communities, each with an industry or two to provide employment, stores, schools, recreational facilities and also with enough ground around the houses so that families can raise a good deal of their foodstuffs or carry on other home projects.

We were discussing this plan in my consultant group of young adults, and one of the young men suggested that the ideal would be communities where there are people practicing different types of skills so that youngsters can enlarge their grasp of these. He himself grew up in such a community and before he entered college could have supported himself quite well through one of several mechanical arts learned from parents or neighbors. I can think of no better preparation for an uncertain future. As for the cost of farm resettlement and new communities, it could hardly be more than to land men on Mars and could hardly be as much as the cost of our recent military ventures. In human terms, a program of this kind could be the saving of our society and freedoms.

Now to wind up the questions I put to my young cooperators.

Agreement and disagreement were very nearly even in the response to the statement of a college psychiatrist that a main cause of today's discontent is that young people feel there is no one they can trust. "They don't believe anything their parents say, they don't believe anything the authorities say, and they don't believe all that their contemporaries say." However, only a handful indicated that this applied to them individually, one of those who did so adding that there were people whose integrity he trusts but not their judgment.

The rest all listed categories of persons they themselves trusted, ranging from a single boy friend or girl friend or pal of the same sex to long rosters which included parents and other relatives, some teachers, usually younger ones, maybe a minister, and friends galore. Several said they trusted everyone until a person showed himself or herself to be untrustworthy. This indicated that lack of trust is not as general as even my young cooperators conceived it to be, an excellent sign for the future, for there can be no love without trust and children can't become whole individuals unless there is someone in their lives whom they trust.

As I talked with young people, I had found considerable concern lest males were becoming feminine and females masculine. So I asked you whether you considered this to be true or untrue and, if true, whether you thought it harmful, beneficial or immaterial.

The idea was rated untrue by a considerable majority, with most of the minority who thought it true considering it harmful, and the number considering it either beneficial or immaterial running about even. Teen-age girls, who gave the biggest majority to "untrue," commented that "the rules are artificial only," "it's only in appearance, that is to say dress," "it doesn't matter because if people want to be weird, let them, they are only hurting themselves," and "I don't think it's true but it would be harmful if it were. A man still has to be a man and a woman a woman."

Of girls twenty and over, who came next in line in the ratio of those voting "untrue," a number expressed the opinion that while it isn't true as yet there is a tendency that way. "Not reversed but changing. Women are becoming more aggressive." "Not reversed but I think they are coming closer together." "It's not far enough along yet but I believe it would be harmful. Girls need to feel respected, loved and protected by a man who can meet masculinity standards." Those who think it is occurring and is beneficial made remarks like "It's great! We've become people, not just male-female dichotomies." From girls twenty and over who think it is occurring and is harmful, there were such comments as: "The girls aren't changing as much as boys. I hate feminine boys." "The men are not becoming men, so the women will be the tough ones." "People are failing to fill traditional roles; this is mainly due to the fact that in parental generations the male has been played down. I believe in equalizing the sexes but not to the point where they are eliminated or meaningless. If people, male or female, fail to assume their roles there will be a breakdown of the entire social structure."

Teen-age boys felt that the change was only in the women, and those who commented considered it harmful. Males twenty and over mostly checked "untrue" with such comments as: "They've lasted this long and they'll stay this way." "I haven't been conscious of my role switching. I'd rather fight than switch! So would most people, most deeply." One who checked yes said, "I think happiness requires males to be in the dominant role, though I do not in any way imply tyranny. The American male is emasculating himself."

I think this is a very important question, though I agree with those who feel that changes in appearance don't matter, at least the ones affected to date by males. Very manly men of the past have worn lace and silk, satin and velvet of gorgeous colors. I have always thought it a pity that, with the nineteenth century, Western men put aside their fine feathers and clamped themselves into wool, drab colors and styles that must be horribly hot in summer; and certainly men are as much entitled to take full advantage of the hair nature has blessed them with as women are.

What I would hate would be to see the chivalrous, protective attitude toward women that good men have had up to this time vanish from the world. After all, we are physically weaker, and if we are honest we must admit that the rights and privileges American women take for granted are ours purely by the sufferance of the men. Perhaps the most unfortunate women in our society today, even more unfortunate than the prostitutes whom they hold up as examples of honesty to the rest of womankind, are the new feminists who are trying to foment a war between the sexes. In an attempt to make a case against the masculine world, they have been claiming that wicked males have enslaved American women in kitchens and behind typewriters, to serve the males' own selfish purposes. As though at some point all American girls are herded into pens and sold off to the highest bidders.

I think the malcontents are doing our sex no service in heaping scorn on secretarial work, which is useful, honorable and well paid, and many times has opened the way to still higher things; and on the housewifely arts, in which I myself have found a pleasure and fulfillment that I wouldn't have missed for anything. They would do much better, I believe, to urge young girls who have dreams of individual achievement to acquire the skills they will need to realize them instead of rushing into early marriages, then blaming the male sex for their frustrations and dissatisfactions. After all, how many brides do *you* know who were dragged to the altar, kicking and screaming?

I agree with the girls who think it a good thing for marriage to be more of a partnership and that there should be a sharing of household duties when the wife is contributing to the exchequer. It doesn't detract from a husband's masculinity to do the marketing, change the baby, wipe dishes or be able to get a meal when his wife is indisposed. But I also agree with my young male cooperator who thinks that the husband should retain the dominant role, though not in a tyrannical sense, as long as women continue to bear children.

That may not always be the case. Science is drawing closer to the ability to gestate human embryos in test tubes, as described by Aldous Huxley in his startlingly prophetic book, *Brave New World*, first published back in 1932, and if that is allowed to come about, it will make an entirely different ball game. I suggest that members of the younger generation read it and decide if that is the kind of world that they will like if they allow it to come into being.

But as things are today and for at least the foreseeable future, the male parent has the responsibility for the family, and that is not a light thing. I have functioned in both roles, as provider and homekeeper, and I can assure you that providing involves much more strain and worry than housekeeping does. It is no mystery to me why the average wife outlives her husband. A second point is that children must have a strong father figure in order to develop normal attitudes toward life. It is also true, as several of the girls have pointed out, that women want manly men and end by despising the ones they can dominate.

The way for a girl to achieve independence and be mistress of her fate is to prepare for some profession or specialty and stick with it. There need be no conflict between career and marriage. Since this century began, countless women have attained distinction in some line of their own while making husbands happy and rearing fine children. It's a matter of organizing, and the woman who is poor at that isn't likely to be a big success in any role.

The dual role is easier today than it used to be. When I was a young career woman, etiquette demanded that a female employee should retire when a pregnancy began to show. Nowadays female executives can go to the hospital directly from the office, if they choose to work up to the last minute. With families limited to two children, it will be easier still, and it will also be more desirable for a wife and mother to have something meaningful to occupy her after her two children no longer need her intensive care.

Advance planning also helps. A young wife I know has completed her training for her specialty, but she and her husband have decided that she should work at it for a year or more before becoming pregnant, and that is wise. It isn't work she can do at home, and she wants to stay at home while her children are small. On-the-job experience will be valuable when the time comes to take up her specialty again. I hope it won't be the lot of any of you girls to be widowed with young children to support and rear alone, or to be among the 50 per cent or so whose marriages now are ending in divorce. But today's smart girl will prepare herself for any contingency.

I think this pretty well covers the really pressing problems you have brought up, and let me say again that this exchange has been a marvelous experience for me, so many of my young helpers have shown so much maturity, perceptiveness and evidence of serious thought in replies to my questions. It has only been necessary for me to sort out from the wide variety of opinions and comments the ones which, from my own experience, observation and studies, are most in accord with the facts of life as I have known it. Many would differ from me on certain points, and that is their right. It has been my great privilege to take part in this exchange, and I think it would be wonderful if there could be many face-to-face discussions between the generations on these subjects which, so you have told me, are most perplexing for today's girls. Let's work on it!

With heartfelt thanks to all my helpers for your interest, cooperation and beautiful honesty,

Your friend always,
GLADYS SHULTZ

The Young People's Questionnaire

From Gladys Denny Shultz
Garrison, N. Y. 10524

Dear Cooperator:

You will probably groan at the idea of filling out another questionnaire, but your frank answers to the questions below will help me very much in writing a book on the order of my *Letters to Jane* (used in many colleges and high schools during the past twenty years) but designed for today's young people and conditions. Though the book will be intended for girls, I would like the male slant and will appreciate it if male cooperators will give their views on all the subjects. Please feel free to enlarge upon response, if necessary using the backs of the sheets. You need not sign your name, and return to me directly in the enclosed stamped, addressed envelope will insure anonymity.

Male ☐ Female ☐ Age ☐

Specify grade, or college class, or how many years of schooling if no longer attending.

I. What do you consider the three most critical questions facing girls in the teens today, in order of their importance? (As kind of education, career choices, love and sex life, general social conditions, etc.)

    1.

    2.

    3.

II. From what you hear and observe among people you know, what do you consider the most serious mistakes made by:

    1. Parents of your generation (not necessarily your own)?
    2. Present-day education?
    3. Society in its attitudes toward and treatment of the young?

III. When or if you have children of your own, which of your own parents' procedures do you think you will:

    1. Try to emulate (specify).
    2. Try to avoid (specify).
    3. Do you keep still about your real views on moral and social matters for fear of hurting your parents? Yes ☐ No ☐

IV. At what age, or grade in school, or stage of maturity (as measured by performance in carrying responsibilities) do you think a girl should be allowed to run her own life without adult interference?

Do you think that an offspring's being dependent on parents financially, or living under the parental roof, entitles parents to expect compliance with certain rules of behavior, as hours to get in at night, etc.?   Yes ☐   No ☐

V. For some time now we have been deluged with pronouncements, mostly from older people, about what young people think and want. Following are some statements of this kind. Will you please check the boxes which deal with attitudes, according to those of groups you are acquainted with, and then your personal reactions. (Please have in mind that these statements have been culled from periodicals, speeches and discussions and do not necessarily represent the writer's impressions or views.)

Statement 1. The younger generation has thrown traditional moral concepts and rules governing sex behavior out the window. Nothing is considered wrong as long as individuals don't hurt others, do what they do in private so as not to offend others, and don't cause concern to their friends. (As by getting hung up on drugs or liquor or sex, etc.)

Appendix: The Questionnaires

Believe that most of the people I know would:

Agree ☐   Disagree ☐

Statement 2, by a college psychiatrist, that a main cause of discontent is that today's young people feel there is no one they can trust. "They don't believe anything their parents say, they don't believe anything the authorities say, and they don't believe all that their contemporaries say." Taken as a general statement, do you:

Agree ☐   Disagree ☐

Is there anyone *you* trust?   Yes ☐   No ☐   If yes, specify nature of the relationship or relationships.

What must older people do to gain the trust of younger ones?

Statement 3.   The great majority of college students and many high schoolers have tried marijuana at least once and a considerable proportion of college students have experimented with a psychedelic or hallucigenic drug. In your observation and experience do you consider this: True ☐   Untrue ☐

If you yourself have never tried marijuana or any of the drugs described just above is it because:

A. You consider it morally wrong?   Yes ☐   No ☐
B. You fear it might harm you?   Yes ☐   No ☐
C. You never had the chance?   Yes ☐   No ☐
D. You didn't really want to?   Yes ☐   No ☐
E. You were afraid of being caught?   Yes ☐   No ☐
F. You knew your parents would disapprove? Yes ☐   No ☐

Statement 4, by a recent graduate at an alumnae meeting of her college: "It is ridiculous for colleges to have rules designed to protect the virtue of girl students because most of those entering colleges today will have lost their virginity while still in high school." Thinking of the girls you know would you say that this statement probably is:

A. Largely true?   ☐
B. Greatly exaggerated?   ☐
C. Untrue?   ☐

Do you feel that there are other reasons for colleges to abolish rules regulating social behavior? If yes, what are they?

Statement 5. Boys today do not expect girls to be virgins and don't think any the less of them if they aren't. Generally speaking this is: True ☐   Untrue ☐

A. The foregoing presumably would apply to girls in general. When it comes to marriage do you think the average man would prefer a virgin or at least a girl who had slept only with him?
                Yes ☐   No ☐

B. If you agree that the old value placed upon virginity until marriage is outmoded, will you please check the items below which in your opinion fit the new moral code:

1. Intercourse should be limited to a steady boy friend with whom the girl considers herself to be in love.
          Yes ☐   Not necessarily ☐

2. It is considered all right for a girl to:
   a. Have intercourse with any boy she likes well enough to date.   Yes ☐   No ☐
   b. Have intercourse on a first date if she feels like it.
            Yes ☐   No ☐
   c. Initiate intimacies with a new date if he doesn't.
            Yes ☐   No ☐

3. What is the responsibility of the boy if a girl becomes pregnant:
   a. As a result of sex relations in a steady, love relationship?
   b. As a result of casual sex, with a girl to whom it was no novelty?

Statement 6, by a famous anthropologist, that what young people today are demanding is legitimization of the things they want to do. "They want the president of the college against which they are demonstrating to come out and march with them. . . . They want the college to say it is okay to use their dormitory rooms for lovemaking and they want their parents to let them use the playroom." Would you say that this statement is:
        Accurate in general ☐   Not true at all ☐
Does it represent your own feeling?   Yes ☐   No ☐
If no, would you please state your feeling briefly.

If your answer to the last question was yes, do you think it should be made legitimate for parents also to "make love" with others than their lawful mates openly and under the family roof?

Yes ☐   No ☐

If your answer was no, please state your reasons briefly.

Statement 7. That among college girls there is widespread use of the pill or other contraceptive device. Would you estimate this to be true of:

A. The majority of girls you know ☐
B. Some but not many   ☐
C. None   ☐

Statement 8. I am told that today's young people don't want to read or hear anything about past history or even what has happened in the last twenty or thirty years. Do you:

Agree ☐   Disagree ☐

If you believe this to be true of many of the people you know, will you explain briefly why you think it is?

VIII. If girls and women, freed of the risk of an unwanted pregnancy by ever safer and surer contraceptive devices, should claim the same freedom men have traditionally enjoyed in sex, do you think this will make any difference in traditional male attitudes toward women, as protectiveness, respect, etc.? Yes ☐   No ☐ Will you briefly explain your answer?

IX. Is it your belief, contrary to the eight statements above, that actually there has been little change in moral conduct; that young people today are simply doing openly the things their forebears used to do *sub rosa*?   Yes ☐   No ☐

X. Marriage, as a sacrament binding "until death do us part," is under attack as well as traditional morals. Would you express your opinion of the following alterations that have been suggested:

1. Before committing themselves to lifelong fidelity in a civil or religious ceremony, a couple would live together for a period of time —two years has been suggested—but refrain from having children. At the end of the period they would either marry or separate without

the trouble and expense of a divorce. A good idea ☐   Not so good ☐   If you consider it not so good, please give reasons.

2. The sacramental aspect of marriage would be dropped altogether in favor of a legal contract, as in a business connection, for five or ten years, to be terminated at expiration without court proceedings if one or both want out, or renewed for another limited period. Good idea ☐   Not so good ☐   If not so good, please give reasons.

3. Would you prefer to rear your children in an environment which emphasizes marriage and the good of the family above individual freedom and desires? Yes ☐   No ☐   If your answer was yes, have you any suggestions for ways by which your generation may reverse the trend toward divorce and family breakups?

XI. There appears to be considerable concern on college campuses lest masculine and feminine roles are changing, with males supposedly becoming more effeminate and females more masculine. Do you think the sex roles are indeed in process of becoming reversed?
Yes ☐   No ☐
If your answer was yes, do you think the trend is: Harmful ☐   Beneficial ☐   Doesn't matter ☐   Please briefly state the reason for your answer.

XII. There is an impression among older people that today's younger generation knows all there is to know about sex and could very probably instruct its elders. Do you feel that there are areas in the field of sex and morals in which not all young people *are* fully informed and which should be discussed in a book for girls in the late high school and college years? If so, won't you tell me what they are? And thank you very much for your help.

GLADYS DENNY SHULTZ
Garrison, N.Y. 10524

The Adults' Questionnaire

FROM GLADYS DENNY SHULTZ
Garrison, N.Y. 10524

DEAR COOPERATOR:

I am working on a book on the order of my *Letters to Jane* (used in many high schools and colleges during the past twenty years) but designed for today's young people and conditions. Your frank answers to the following questions will be very helpful. Please feel free to enlarge upon responses and to add comments and topics, if necessary using the backs of the sheets. Direct return to me in the enclosed stamped, addressed envelope will insure anonymity.

Age ☐   Sex ☐   Number of years of schooling ☐   Degrees, if any: _____ Please specify basis of your special interest in young people—as parent, grandparent, teacher, worker with youth groups, etc.

I. Which of the following statements most nearly expresses your feeling about the "new" youth?

A. The sit-ins, drug experimentation, wanton destruction, repudiation of traditional moral and sex standards and challenges to authority are confined to a few; the great majority are behaving themselves as well (recognizing that each generation develops its own way of doing things) as we did, in terms of ours, and will carry out our basic principles, though perhaps in somewhat modified form.   Agree ☐   Disagree ☐

B. The revolt of youth is wholesome and good. The young have been forced to behave spectacularly because their elders haven't listened, and the demonstrations are bringing about needed reforms.　　　　　Agree ☐　　Disagree ☐

C. The phenomena mentioned in Statement A are symptoms of a degeneration in the moral fiber of our society which, if not checked, threatens the survival of our system of government and society.　　　　　Agree ☐　　Disagree ☐

If none of the foregoing represents your view, won't you state what it is.

II. Whether or not you agree with Statement C just above, is it your feeling that the fault lies with:

A. Bad examples set by adults with regard to drinking, sex behavior, marriage break-ups, contempt for law, etc.?
　　　　　　　　Yes ☐　　No ☐

B. The permissiveness prevailing in much child training and educational theory during the past two decades?
　　　　　　　　Yes ☐　　No ☐

C. Lowering of the general moral climate, as evidenced by the explosion of raw sex in reading matter, movies and theater; violence on television; malfeasance by public officials; repudiation of obligations, as illegal strikes by civil service employees engaged in essential services?　　　　　Yes ☐　　No ☐

D. Frustration and justified resentment by youth over Vietnam and the draft rules?　　Yes ☐　　No ☐

E. Serious failure on the part of schools and colleges to give young people what they need?
　　　　　　　　Yes ☐　　No ☐

F. Anxiety of middle-class parents and society to give our youths "advantages," whether or not they have merited or want them, thereby becoming patsies for spoiled youngsters who don't know what they do want and have learned to keep the grown-ups off base by escalating unrealistic demands?
　　　　　　　　Yes ☐　　No ☐

G. Deliberate beaming of advertising at children and teen-agers —beginning with box tops and extending now to automobiles— which has given them a false sense of importance and their right

to dictate in matters for which they have no personal responsibility?
Yes □   No □

H. The breaking down of paternal power through radio and TV serials and movies which present Dad as a bumbling idiot, forever having to be extricated by his clever wife and children from the messes he gets himself into?
Yes □   No □

Please add to the above list as you see fit; and in addition to marking yes or no in the right-hand boxes, won't you please put check marks to the left of any factors which you consider particularly important in bringing about the present crises.

III. Margaret Mead has been quoted as saying that today's teen-agers are demanding not merely to run their own lives but to have the things they want to do legitimatized. "They want the president of the college they are demonstrating against to come out and march with them. . . . They want the college to say it is okay to use their dormitory rooms for love-making and they want their parents to let them use the playroom." Among the young people you know, would you say this is true of: The majority □
A small number □   None at all □

Which of the following expresses your own feeling?

If my daughter is going to engage in intercourse, I would rather she did it at home than in a car parked where police or a sex deviate might find her. Yes □   No □

Whatever my son or daughter may be doing outside, I feel I have a right to keep my home free of conduct I disapprove of.
Yes □   No □

Other reaction, or further comment if you wish.

IV. Colleges are rather rapidly abandoning the *in loco parentis* role they have formerly played and are more and more leaving it to students to regulate their social conduct according to their individual lights. As you feel about matters now, would you want to send a seventeen-year-old girl whose welfare is important to you to a college which:

A. Assumes no responsibility for policing student behavior off

[223]

campus (such as holding a pot-smoking party in a motel, etc.) or for the hour when students shall be in at night?

Yes ☐   No ☐

B. Allows boys to stay overnight in girls' dormitories and vice versa? (I do not refer here to the new type of dormitory for both sexes, with separate sleeping quarters, but to overnight stay in the sleeping quarters of the opposite sex.)

Yes ☐   No ☐

C. Sanctions off-campus "shacking up" of unmarried couples?

Yes ☐   No ☐

D. Outfits with the kind of contraceptive device considered best suited to her needs, in its medical clinic, any coed who wants one?

Yes ☐   No ☐

E. Would you want to send her to a college which permits some or all the foregoing for juniors and seniors, but imposes some regulations on the activities of freshmen and sophomore?

Yes ☐   No ☐

If you have had any experience of the above changes, won't you please give your estimate of the effect on student conduct and attention to studies.

V. Where college administrators have yielded to "nonnegotiable" demands under threat of violence or to prevent violence, do you consider the results to have been to:

A. Serve the best interests of the institution, the students and higher education generally?

Yes ☐   No ☐

B. Lead to further disruption and more outrageous demands?

Yes ☐   No ☐

VI. When my son enrolled at Harvard in the fall of 1948, I had to sign a bond committing myself to pay up to $500 for any damage he might do to college property, and it had to be countersigned by someone not a member of the immediate family. (I figured this precaution stemmed from Harvard's more than 300 years of experience not only with high-spirited youth but with the kind of parents whose sons are allowed to reach college age without having become civilized.)

A. If parents of young people who have done deliberate and serious damage to college buildings had been required to pay for the cleaning up and repairs, do you think they might have had a different attitude toward their youngsters' actions?

Yes □   No □

B. Do you agree with the students cited just above, and, one judges, with their parents as well, that there should be no unpleasant consequences to their vandalism, because their cause is just? Yes □   No □

C. If you feel that parents have some responsibility in the unlawful or destructive conduct of their young, what do you consider it to be?

VII. Do you hesitate to express your views about sex, ethics and the rights of other people than the demonstrators in the presence of the young, lest they consider you square and a member of the Establishment?   Yes □   No □

VIII. Would you estimate, as nearly as you can, to what extent your opinions and feelings about these matters are influenced by:

A. Religious or home training   %
B. What you read and see on stage, screen or TV   %
C. Personal experience and observation   %

IX. If the new developments on the youth scene—drug-taking, overturn of traditional moral standards, involvement in radical movements, etc.—are affecting or you fear may affect someone in your family or school district or acquaintance, I wish you would describe the situation and tell me what you think about it. This questionnaire is being distributed by people I know to friends of theirs, to whose identity I haven't the slightest clue, and the distributors will not see the questionnaires after they are filled out. If I should use any of the personal experiences in my book, I will alter minor details further to prevent the possibility of identification.

[225]

X. If you have found effective ways of keeping communication open with the young people you are involved with, or in other ways have had experiences which it would help other adults to know about, won't you please describe.

Thank you very much for your cooperation.

GLADYS DENNY SHULTZ
Garrison, N.Y. 10524